How To Find and Select the Perfect Mate

Rodger L. Winn

ISBN: 0-9969184-1-8
ISBN-13: 978-09969184-1-1

DEDICATION

This book is dedicated to my young friends who have not yet found their perfect mates, and to Margie Logan, the original inspiration for this book.

Cover: Casey Winn proposing to Mayuko Abe in Golden Gate Park, San Francisco. Photo by Joel Gutierrez.

CONTENTS

1

INTRODUCTION

Surely the selection of a mate is one of the most serious and difficult of the tasks we humans have to face while passing through this life, yet it is one of those for which we are least prepared. The goal of this book is to provide a useful understanding of what it is that you really want in a mate, and to offer some suggestions for the search and selection of that mate.

This book is intended to help put into words some of the things you might think about, perhaps subconsciously, when you try to find a mate. It is my belief that if you could do a better job analyzing and describing what you want or don't want in a mate, you should be better able to locate and attract a person who is just right for you.

Most of us were raised with the idea that marriage is what we should want when we grow up, because this is what the majority of adults have done for centuries in our western culture. The institution of marriage seems to be failing, however, and we need to take a larger view of what is happening. It appears that the marriage format, which was designed so long ago, has trouble fitting into our modern environment. Most books on love and marriage discuss people's behavior and mate selection just from the perspective of psychology or sociology, and don't account for many of the changes that have occurred in our modern society. I would like to present a different approach. Having been a technical salesman for twenty five years, I am going to discuss the pursuit of an ideal mate from a salesman's point of view.

Rather than decide for you what attributes you should look for in a mate, as many authors do, I will try to help you decide for yourself what it is that you want in a mate. You may never have been a salesman yourself, but you certainly have had plenty of experience dealing with salesmen of all types. Everything you have ever bought or sold put you into a sales situation of one kind or another, and I think you will be able to use this personal background and experience to evaluate the ideas I am presenting here.

I am going to use sales analogies all through the book because I think there is a very strong parallel. You are trying to "sell" yourself to a worthwhile potential mate, and also at the same time trying to decide whether or not to "buy" his or her program. When you are in the sales mode trying to sell yourself, you need to carefully analyze the product being sold (you) and figure out where you can find a buyer. When you are in the buying mode, there is information to be gathered, alternatives to be considered, decisions to be made, and risks to be taken, just as in all other buying situations.

This is not a book for dreamers and wishful thinkers. This book will deal with the hard cold facts of the real world we all live in and have to find a mate in. We are surrounded by divorces, unhappy marriages, broken hearts, and lonely single people. We don't need any more proof that finding a mate is a very difficult task. It is my goal to help you be more analytical about the task of mate selection, so you will be better prepared to actually find and select that perfect mate.

Author's Note:

The idea for this book originated in about 1970 when I had four excellent roommates over a five year span. I was in my 30's at the time and had been dating heavily for years, but still had not found a mate that I was willing to marry. It dawned on me that finding a roommate was pretty easy compared to how difficult it was to find a spouse, and I started thinking about why this was so. The subject swirled around in my brain for about 20 years until I started to commit my ideas to paper in the early 90's. I decided that I could put together some thoughts about marriage that could take advantage of my experience as a salesman, equating the decision process of selecting a mate to the decision process of buying and selling in the other parts of our lives.

The book publishers were not interested in making this into a commercial book, so the manuscript has sat on my computer through 4 generations of computers without ever seeing daylight. Everyone with whom I discussed it, however, thought it was a good way to look at marriage and asked for a copy. It is now 2016 and I am confident enough that this still makes sense that I am willing to share my ideas. I have reviewed the whole thing and made a few changes, but it is essentially the same as I wrote it in the 90's, and I think it is still valid.

2

WHY MARRY?

Marriage has been the ceremony that formalizes the family as the social entity responsible for creating and raising children. However, support for marriage from the church and the state are no longer the controlling forces, and too many marriages are unsatisfactory or break down altogether. The world is already overpopulated so the need for more children is no longer compelling, and many people will choose to not become parents. But with or without children, many of us will still want the comfort and security of having that very special partner, and will make the considerable effort required to find him/her. It won't be easy. We need to understand more about what marriage now means, and how to find a good one.

Marriage is probably the most complex relationship any of us can get ourselves into, yet we get little training, advice, or help in how to do it right. Not surprisingly, half of our marriages end in divorce, and many of the other half are far less than perfect. We need to do better, both as individuals and as a society, at understanding what marriage means in our modern world. Aside from having children, some of the traditional reasons for marriage are no longer valid, and the marriage decision should not be taken lightly.

What is the purpose of marriage anyway, besides being a partnership in child rearing? Is it to provide us with love, sex, companionship, security, a meal ticket, health coverage, maid service, a cook, a bridge partner? I doubt if most people can give a good answer if asked what they want out of marriage. Marriage seems to be something that most of us want but we have a hard time describing what "it" is that we want.

As I look at this from the perspective of a salesman, I have to say this is crazy. When people go to buy something, they generally have a pretty good idea about what it is they want to buy. As the price goes up, the buyer gets more careful. When the price gets really high, both parties sign a purchase agreement or a contract stating exactly what is expected of and by both parties. In business, they only let a special group of experienced, trained people do the buying, a group typically designated as the purchasing department.

What happens in marriage, by contrast? You are "buying" into a long term commitment, in probably the single biggest decision anybody ever makes, and what do we know about marriage? Not enough, I'm sure. Including those who have been married before and are hoping to do better the next time.

What do you expect to get out of a marriage? How would you know if you have gotten a good one or not? What would you do if you didn't?

In the old days, there were lots of factors that helped keep a marriage together, so that marriage really meant "till death do us part". In our society today there are too many other interests and competing lifestyles trying to pull us apart, and there is no social stigma attached to divorce, no pressure from the church, or even from our families, to force us to stay together. As a result of all this, people can get into marriage too easily, without enough concern for what happens if things don't work out perfectly. And even if we do try to marry correctly, lots of people will back out of marriage for what used to be considered minor problems. No-fault divorce over "irreconcilable differences" is not much of an obstacle to divorce.

Why do you want to get married anyway? Marriage is work; everybody says so. If this is true, then you certainly want to get properly compensated for your effort, don't you? What is it you want to get out of a marriage?

For many people, sex is a major reason for getting married. Having a steady, safe sex partner is all the more important in an era like the '90's, when AIDS and other sexually transmitted diseases are such a problem.

If this is your goal, however, there are always alternatives. In addition to the sex magazines and sex videos, there is now discussion about cybersex on the computer networks. Newsweek even carried an article about it, and quotes Lisa Palac, editor of *Future Sex*, a magazine about high-tech sex, "Some of the best sex I've ever had has been with myself," she says. "We have to break out of this idea that having sex alone makes you a loser." On the other hand, as Linda Sunshine says in *Dating Iron John & Other Pleasures*, her very funny satire, "No matter how much you may enjoy having sex in the privacy of your own bathroom, sex can be even better when you do it with another person."

But if sex is one of your objectives in marriage, you had better make sure you marry a person with whom you are compatible on other issues as well, as will be discussed in a following chapter.

A couple that is blissfully happy probably has good sex. A couple that fights a lot probably has some sex. And a couple in divorce proceedings probably has no sex. Plot a curve for yourself showing these relationships, and what does it tell you? What it clearly illustrates is that if the two of you don't get along well, you're not going to have much sex.

Some people get married hoping to get rid of the loneliness of being single. If this is your objective, you need to stop and analyze this very carefully. We all know what it means to be lonely, because we've all been lonely at some time or other, and it's not a really good feeling. But it's not a very bad feeling either, compared to some of the other feelings you could have if you get into a bad marriage.

Obviously, what we all want to do is trade in our feelings of loneliness as a single person for the feelings of bliss and belonging that we expect to accompany the wedding vows. This is like the movie with the happy ending, based on Hollywood stereotypes and unrealistic expectations. What does reality have to offer?

Not nearly so many happy endings as we would hope. Some people really do have good marriages, however. The *L. A. Times* had an interesting article about a number of couples who married right and have been happy together for years. In fact, Sylviane Sydney Kitchen of Galveston, Texas was so tired of hearing people complain about their spouses on all the big talk shows that she organized a competition for October of 1993, the winner of which was to be crowned "America's Perfect Couple." Other marriages aren't so good, however, and the flip side of this coin is that the least happy people are those in unhappy marriages.

In my opinion, marriage is much more difficult now than it used to be for four reasons:

1) women's lib,
2) modern technology,
3) the difficulty in finding a compatible mate, and,
4) our anxiety about the future.

1) The first is women's lib. Before women's lib, not many women had the chance to develop and advance on their own, and they settled into an existence where the husband was the primary breadwinner. The marriage survived because the husband and wife had fairly well defined roles to play, and they accepted those roles. The issue is not whether it was fair or unfair; what mattered was that everybody knew their roles and acted accordingly.

Since the onset of women's lib and the equality of women, it is no longer so clear as to who is to do what. Because the woman is now contributing to the family income, she feels that she is entitled to a bigger say in how it is spent. That means constant negotiation. Because she works as well as he, it seems only fair that he contribute to the household chores. Since that's not the way it used to be, that also means constant negotiation. When the rules aren't clear, it's very hard to decide whether you want to play or not.

2) The second reason is due to technology and our modern lifestyles. Men used to need a wife to do the cooking, do the laundry, and keep the house clean. These were considered women's jobs and most men didn't even want to know how to do them. Now, however, men no longer need a cook because of today's microwave technology, super-market deli's, and fast food outlets. Laundromats and cleaners take care of those other needs, and even a man can run the vacuum cleaner once in a while. So who needs a wife?

On the other hand, women used to need a man because of his income earning potential; there were few high paying jobs for women. They needed a man who could handle the heavier tasks around the homestead and who was able to fix things. And perhaps as important a reason as any, social custom required that a woman be accompanied by a man in many circumstances. Clearly all this has changed, so who needs a husband?

3) The third reason why marriage is so difficult now is that it is so much harder to find a compatible mate in a larger, more impersonal world full of strangers. One of the major requirements for compatibility is that you and your mate share the same view of the world, and have the same values and interests, and having similar backgrounds makes this more likely. The bigger the city, the greater the probability that the people you meet will have backgrounds which are quite different from yours, and the harder it is to find a person who is compatible.

4) The fourth reason has to do with our current levels of frustration and anxiety compared with our expectations about life and happiness. Life is so much better than it was in the past that we ought to be able to call the present an era of relative happiness. But we don't, says Peggy Noonan, who worked as a writer for Dan Rather, Ronald Reagan, and George Bush. Rather than what should be happiness, she says, the fraying of our social fabric, the decay of our financial security, and the decline in our personal safety have us feeling anxiety instead. There is no margin for error anymore.

Some people are hoping that marriage is the silver bullet that will make everything turn out right, but I think this is clearly open to question. Getting married is a big decision which causes some significant changes in your life, and has to be carefully analyzed on an individual basis.

Let's take an example from a sales scenario to use as an analogy. The decision to buy your first car is similar to the marriage decision, in that both require a step into the unknown. Imagine living in a city that has relatively good bus and train service and analyzing your lifestyle to see if it makes sense to buy a car. Since in reality you have probably been through this scenario already, you know that buying a car will allow you to avoid all the problems due to the bus and train, but you also know that it will introduce a whole new set of problems associated with owning a car. Ask anyone who lives in New York City. Switching from using the bus and train to owning a car is not necessarily a good deal. Switching from being single to being married is also not necessarily a good deal, as more and more people are deciding.

Traditionally, marriage made good sense. The hard or dangerous tasks, (hunting, warfare, heavy work) were usually assigned to the men. Children require a long time to develop, and need lots of attention in the process, and this was done by the women. The family was the most workable social group to accomplish this whole task in most of the societies we're familiar with.

Today's situation is totally different. Women can perform almost all of the jobs that men can, so they don't have to depend on men for an income. The social pressure on women to have a husband has disappeared, and women can get their own credit ratings and establish their own businesses. Our whole attitude towards pre-marital sex has changed as well, so people don't have to be married to have a sex life. (There may be religious groups that will strongly disapprove of all this, but their loss of influence is also one of the changes that has occurred.)

Because our basic survival needs are now pretty well taken care of, an important purpose for having a mate now and in the future will be to satisfy our emotional needs. Historically, people used to get a lot of emotional support from an extended family, but now many of us have moved away from the other family members. Today, we live in a changing society amongst a crowd of strangers who really don't care a whole lot about how things are going for us personally. Our jobs aren't guaranteed anymore, so we can't even get a sense of security out of going to the same old workplace year after year. And the welfare office certainly isn't motivated to give us any emotional support, we know that. So who is going to give a damn about you, anyway. Nobody.

That's why you get married. Marriage means that somebody does care about you. It means that somebody is willing to make a commitment to provide you with love and support, to be your friend and partner for the rest of your life. When it is done right, marriage should give you a tremendous feeling of well being.

The problem is that marriage requires knowledge, understanding, sharing and sacrifice, and in marriage you have to give as well as get. Many of us are not very good at providing this level of emotional support, so we enter into a marriage relationship under-qualified to fulfill the duties of the job.

In our society, the laws regarding contracts have evolved to the point where lawyers get paid millions to generate and interpret contracts. Anybody who does anything serious always has a contract that clearly specifies what the benefits and obligations are for all the parties involved. The main piece of advice we are all given regarding contacts is to "read the fine print". When it comes to marriage, we don't even have the large print. The closest we come to defining marriage is our promise to love, honor and obey. There is no assurance anywhere that the marriage is a good and fair deal for either party, much less for both parties, which is what you would hope.

It would help if you could find a training class for people who are planning to get married, with a test at the end to show your fitness for marriage. Think about this: You have to pass a test in order to drive, or to practice any of the professions. You have to pass a test to sell real estate, or to teach English. But you don't have to prove to anybody that you know what marriage is all about, or that you know how to handle it. What else do we allow in our society that has a 50% failure rate?

Because we are starting to realize the high personal and social cost of all these divorces, organizations, particularly some churches, are now providing these kinds of services to help people get married more successfully.

Lots of people, however, are choosing not to marry, and being single is becoming more and more accepted as a legitimate lifestyle choice. For those who chose to remain single, the singles magazines have even coined the new designation "single independent" to distinguish themselves from those who are single but would rather not be. Since these two groups have different objectives, it is important that you decide which is the group you fall into, and choose your potential candidates accordingly.

Clearly the pressures are tremendous in the two career family of today. In the old time "classic" marriage of 20, 30,

50 years ago, the husband and wife each had an eight hour a day job. His was outside the home, hers was inside the home. But in our modern two income family, the woman also goes to work outside the home. So who does the home job? In lots of households, it is still the woman who does all or most of the housework, which means she could have, in effect, a very long work day. If they share the housework equally, they might both have the equivalent of 12 hour work days by the time the kids are put to bed. It's easy to see how husband and wife can get on each others' nerves because there is so much to be done that there is very little leisure time in which to enjoy life.

Ongoing polls by the *Roper Organization*, a New York based opinion research firm, indicate that men talk a good game about helping with the chores, but their actions don't quite match their words. Men do grocery shopping, cooking and washing dishes. But the more unpleasant the job, the less men do it. Studies have shown that toilet scrubbing, floor washing, laundry, and oven cleaning are things that men would rather leave for the females to do.

Women also resent how the childcare duties are shared. Women generally do far more of the daily chores, the ones that can't be put off, such as bathing a child, cooking or arranging to get to the doctor.

Even in those situations where the husband does his share of the duties, the woman carries most of the family's psychological burden. She's the one who worries about the children, plans the meals, and maintains the household. Women don't think they can totally concentrate on their careers, because when emergencies occur, like going to the doctor, they are the ones who have to take the responsibility for getting it done.

A Roper survey for Virginia Slims found that women's attitudes toward men have deteriorated over the last several decades. In 1970, 30% of women believed that most men are basically selfish and self centered. In 1990, more than 40% believed that statement to be true.

This complicated lifestyle and level of frustration for the women has some significant negative consequences for the men. One of the letters to Dear Abby explains it very well.

Dear Abby: My wife and I went together throughout college. We have been married 12 years and have three children, ages 5, 7 and 9. Now that we are older (we are both in our 30s), my sex drive seems to be increasing, and my wife's sex drive is definitely decreasing. We are both in good health and hold down full-time jobs, but on a scale of 1 to 10, our sex life would probably be a 2 (for twice a month).

We discussed the problem and ended up going to a marriage counselor. The counselor suggested that I look for other things in my life for satisfaction. I took his advice, found a new hobby, took up a sport and spent more time with the children. This was very rewarding, but I would still like a more romantic relationship with my wife.

Please don't suggest flowers, candy and the like because I have tried these things with little success. (I also had an affair, and although the immediate gratification was exciting, the guilt that followed was terrible.) Any positive suggestions you can offer would be welcome. Right now I am ... Frustrated.

Dear Frustrated.

Perhaps holding down a full-time job and mothering pre-teen children has left your wife with little energy for anything else.

Have you considered giving her a day off now and then, and helping with the housework and the children? It's also possible that some short vacations without the children could rekindle your sex life.

Another thought: make an appointment for the two of you to see a licensed sex therapist. You both have too much invested in this marriage to let it wither.

I suspect that the reactions to this letter will be quite different for men and for women. Women will probably wonder why, since he apparently has such a good lifestyle and a nice family, he's making such a big fuss. Men, on the other hand, will look at this and wonder why they should get married and have kids if this is what they have to look forward to. Why would a man want to settle for a couple of years of good sex and then 20 years of deprivation because the little woman is "too tired"?

It is understandable that a busy woman could have a hard time trying to keep up with being a mother, a worker and a wife. She has a home and family to focus on, as well as her job, and maybe sex is just not a high priority for her.

Look at it from his point of view, however. He can take up a hobby and learn a new sport all by himself as a bachelor. What he needs from his wife is the sex. Because this man is already married, he has a problem that he can't avoid and it's a problem he will have to find a solution to.

But a man who is single and reads this still has an option as to whether or not to get married. Will a single man want to "buy" into a marriage with this kind of a future? Would you expect a man to take on a lifetime commitment when it satisfies his most basic need for only the first few years of marriage and then becomes less than satisfactory?

If many women are unhappy with marriage, and many men are unhappy with marriage, and half of all the marriages end up in divorce, we're not doing something right. Maybe with more analysis and planning, you can improve the chances of finding happiness in your own personal situation.

The following chapters should help in your search and selection of the right mate, and bring to your attention the significant amount of effort and planning required if you want to have a successful marriage.

2005 update: A new book written this year, *Reason* by Robert Reich sounds very similar to what I wrote in 1990. He says "We now have a great many marriages in which both people work and they are so tired and stressed that the only thing they want to do in bed is sleep." Reich has even coined an acronym for these couples: DINS - double income, no sex.

3

THE FOUR "C"S OF MARRIAGE

I think there are four factors which are necessary in order to assure a good relationship between two partners in today's environment. These are: chemistry, commitment, compatibility, and competence. Think of them as the four "C's" to help you survive through the rough "seas" of marriage.

Chemistry

Chemistry relates to that set of characteristics that causes you to feel emotionally and sexually attracted to each other, so that you want to be together. Chemistry is the fun part of the relationship, but, because the attraction may fade with time, it is not a sufficient condition all by itself. It has to be balanced by several other factors which are just as important and perhaps easier to analyze. Thousands of books have been written about the chemistry part of a relationship, so I will leave the subject of "love" to the other authors.

I will concentrate instead on the other three components that I think will be needed in your plan to find a satisfactory mate and a successful relationship.

Commitment

Marriage requires a commitment that will provide its partners with the security of knowing they are in a long term relationship. It is an anchor of stability in a complex and changing world. But this commitment comes at a cost, which will be discussed in the next chapter.

Compatibility

Compatibility means matching your beliefs and behavior patterns with those of the person you choose for a mate so that you can enjoy each other during many years of marriage. A chapter on compatibility will discuss in detail some of the characteristics you may want to consider in a mate to assure the maximum compatibility between the two of you.

Competence

Competence means that you are able to function in a very complex and competitive world as a fully capable adult, accepting the consequences that are the result of marriage. Competence means that you understand the differences between men and women, and can cope with these differences. It refers to your ability to appreciate and stroke each other, to resolve conflicts, and to avoid violence and compulsive or addictive behaviors. A detailed discussion about competence will be presented in a later chapter.

4

COMMITMENT: THE COST OF MARRIAGE

People who are in love can be so starry-eyed that they envision all the benefits to marriage but they forget to consider the other side of the equation. Nothing in life comes for free, you know. Like everything else, marriage comes at a price. Commitment means that you are willing to pay that price.

If a marriage is good, the benefits are worth the price. If the marriage is not good, and the benefits aren't there, you pay the price anyway. There is no product warranty for marriage, and you can't sue for malpractice or incompetence. If you can't figure out how to improve it, you either suffer or you leave it.

What is the cost of commitment to marriage?

1) Marriage means that you are legally, morally and ethically responsible for your spouse and your children, and this responsibility is part of the price you pay once you commit to a marriage relationship. Marriage is a contract, and this is

how society knows where to assign responsibility for property, legal obligations, and especially the rearing of children.

2) Loss of freedom is another part of the price you have to pay. Your thinking and planning must be in terms of "we" instead of "me". You give up some of your personal choices about how to structure your life in favor of goals that enhance the group benefit. Marriage is like adding a sidecar to your motorcycle. You get decreased flexibility and mobility, but coupled with increased responsibility and obligation. Your control is greatly reduced so you can't navigate with abandon anymore. You have to be much more careful because others get hurt when you crash.

3) Having to compromise should be considered a cost. The more compatible your mate is, the less this part of the cost will be. This is the cost you have the most control over, which is why I will stress compatibility so heavily in this book.

4) Fourth is your opportunity cost. In the financial world, "opportunity cost" is the potential benefit you can't take advantage of because your resources are already tied up. In the context we're discussing here, it is the missed opportunity to date or marry somebody else, or perhaps there is some other opportunity in life you have to miss because you are married. You can minimize this cost by enjoying yourself while single and not getting married until you are really ready.

5) Fifth is the cost of failure. Businesses have to set aside a contingency fund to cover unexpected losses of various kinds, because these invariably occur. In the case of a good marriage, this cost is zero, but in a marriage that fails, this can be a very high cost. With divorces occurring in 50% of

all marriages, this is a cost that can't be ignored. You try to avoid this cost by truly understanding marriage and then marrying the right person.

When you try to get a loan to buy a house, the bank investigates your background very carefully before they give their approval. They want to know for sure that you will keep up your monthly payments for 30 years. A marriage is supposed to last for 30 years also, but the payments have to be made daily.

You can't afford to be casual about your marriage decision, perhaps thinking that you can use your first marriage as practice for your second one. This rarely works, because the divorce rates are even higher for second marriages. And remember, there are no winners in a divorce. There is a sarcastic but true saying in the business world that is appropriate here. "How come there is never enough time to do things right the first time, but there is always time to do it over the second time."

The secret to success in marriage is to do your planning on your way into marriage, not when trying to get out of it. Selecting the right mate, and delaying the decision, are two of the most important elements to include in keeping the "cost" of marriage down.

5

COMPATIBILITY: THE CRITERIA

Almost everything you read about marriage implies that marriage is work. Have you ever thought about what this means? Why should you have to work at marriage? And if you do have to work at it, is there a way to minimize the work? Yes, there is. Pick a mate who's compatible.

When it comes to selecting a mate you've probably heard the statement that "opposites attract". Well, in my opinion that statement refers to how magnets work, not to how people do. The "work" required in marriage occurs because you don't get everything exactly the way you want, and you have to compromise on a lot of things. But small compromises are easier to cope with than big compromises.

The major benefit to being single is that you don't need anybody's approval to do anything, so you don't need to compromise. You can spend your money any way you like, go anywhere you want, do what you choose. When you get married, it is most likely that your mate will not see things exactly your way, certainly not all the time, and it is coping with these differences that creates the work in marriage.

There will probably be some characteristics that you think are absolutely essential in a mate, and you should decide what these are right up front. Perhaps the most well known set of criteria comes from a famous movie from many years ago in which a young lady tells a friend that she wants a man who is "tall, dark and handsome." That's fine, if that's what you want in a mate. Or, you could decide that you want someone who is warm, tender, and caring. Or you could want your mate to be attractive, have a good job, and be a good dancer. Some people will insist that a mate be athletic. A friend of mine said he wanted a woman who was thin, non-smoking, with a college degree. I've had women tell me that they only want a man who has a sense of humor. Whatever it is that you want in a mate, if it is that important to you, put it on your list. (Rich doesn't count; that's on everybody's list.)

Pick three characteristics that define what you want in a mate, three characteristics that you absolutely will not do without. But don't pick any more than three. Any more than that is unworkable and unrealistic. Any other characteristics you might want in a mate should all be minor by comparison to the first three, and these can be used later in the qualification process after you have found a potential candidate. Once you have picked your three absolutely essential criteria, these remaining criteria will help you fine tune your compatibility analysis, which will then help determine success or failure in your pursuit of happiness through marriage.

It would be wrong to think that you are going to get the person you want by changing him or her after you get married. (Look in the mirror: How much are you willing or able to change?) You have to get the compatibility you want by being careful during your selection process.

To explain what I mean about compatibility and why I think it is important, I have listed a number of criteria that I think are components of compatibility. You may decide that some of these are not relevant criteria for you, which is just fine. It's not the criteria on my list that are important anyway; each reader has to make up his/her own list of criteria that will be important in selecting a mate. My list is just to get you thinking about what ought to go on your list.

The experts say that if you hope to have a marriage that will last, there will have to be more to it than just physical attraction, because that will probably subside somewhat with time. You will also have to be friends. This will most likely occur if there is a good match between the two of you on all of the criteria I have listed below. (Or whichever other criteria you select as being relevant for yourself). It does not matter where you position yourself on the scale for any of these criteria; it only matters that you and your mate be at approximately the same position on the scale for each criteria.

I think it is very important to be non-judgmental about these criteria, so try to keep from deciding whether a certain behavior is good or bad. It is only important that you determine where you fall on each scale and try to find a mate who is compatible with you on each of the criteria.

Some people will insist that there is some validity to the long standing piece of conventional wisdom that says that "opposites attract". My theory about compatibility directly contradicts this notion. Whether or not you agree may be a function of how willing you are to compromise and how much you try to avoid conflict. But maybe after you read what I have in mind for each of the criteria, you will agree that you really don't want someone who is "opposite," at least not on these issues.

People will, of course, differ on many, many issues, and some of these do not have to be mentioned because they are so obvious. That's what dating is for, and if the differences are significant, you won't even have a second date. But casual dating is easy. The following analysis is intended to help you verbalize your thoughts when you have reservations about marrying someone and you can't quite put your finger on what the problem is.

Please note that in the following list, I have tried not to make any value judgments about what is a good and/or proper personality trait or behavior pattern. People are entitled to behave any way they want to, and it's not for you to decide how they should behave. Your task is not to mold someone into being the person you want; your task is to find and select someone with whom you are compatible.

What I am trying to explain in the following discussion is that on any given criteria, there is a range of behavior that goes from having none of that criteria to having lots of that criteria. Very few people will fall at the extremes on any of these scales, and there is quite a range over which most of us will find ourselves. Take a look at some of the criteria I've thought of that could be important when you are deciding whether or not someone is right for you. See if you don't agree that what you really want is to have a mate very much like yourself.

Criteria	One end of scale	Other end of scale
Cleanliness	slovenly	super clean
spending money	miserly	spend thrift
modesty	exhibitionist	modest
sharing	self-centered	sharing
culture	unrefined	erudite

Criteria	One end of scale	Other end of scale
honesty	unscrupulous	saintly
family	high involvement	no involvement
kids	no kids	lot of kids
emotions	calm	passionate
decision making	liberated	traditional
personality	child-like	parent-like
sociability	hermit-like	gregarious
religion	non-religious	religious
ambition	complacent	ambitious
looks	unattractive	gorgeous
status	low status	high status
individuality	other-directed	inner-directed
dominance	submissive	controlling
energy level	indolent	hyper-active
intelligence	dumb	brilliant
sex	non-sexual	over-sexed
risk taking	cautious	daring
communication	taciturn	loquacious
organization	unorganized	organized
diligence	undisciplined	persistent
life style	rural	urban

Cleanliness

Let's take the first one on the list, cleanliness, as an example. Having no cleanliness would mean that a person is slovenly, ill-kempt, dirty, messy, etc. If we were to graph this on a linear scale, with slovenly on one end of the scale, on the other end of the cleanliness scale would be someone who is super clean and neat, persnickety, fastidious. I mean cleanliness here in the most general sense. There could be all kinds of situations where cleanliness is an issue, such as personal hygiene, how often you wash the kitchen floor, whether or not you can tolerate dirty dishes in the sink. This could also refer to whether or not you leave magazines on the coffee table, how you make the bed, whether you pick up your socks. Some people would just cringe at the thought of anything less than the utmost cleanliness; others can't be that concerned. I think you can see the need for a pretty good match on this criteria or the cleaner one will always be criticizing the other one.

Spending Money

Let's take a look at the second one on the above list, in two parts: how you spend money, and what you spend it on. Some people are so concerned about saving money that they refrain from spending money on satisfying even their immediate needs. Like the famous Scrooge, they deny themselves far more than most people would consider necessary. This would describe the left end of the scale. On the other end of the scale is the person who not only spends everything he has, but spends it faster than he earns it, and is constantly in debt. Here again these two positions define the extremes on this criteria, and you should be able to place yourself on this scale somewhere between the two extremes. In addition to how you spend money, what you spend your money on will also be an issue. Do you buy a fancy new car or a room addition on your house? Do you take an expensive vacation, or put the money into stocks and bonds? From what I read, money is a major source of conflict in marriage because there is never enough of it. You want to make sure you and your partner have compatible philosophies on how to spend and save it.

Modesty

Would you dance if you were the only couple on the dance floor, or would you wait until the floor was filled with people so you could hide? How would you feel if your mate talks so loudly that he/she can be heard clear across the restaurant? Would you go to a nude beach? Would you mind if your spouse did? Are you willing to change clothes in front of your spouse? Do you tend to not say much in a group, or is it important that your opinion be heard? Some people are exhibitionists, which might not sit well with those who are modest about personal matters. Unless there is a reasonable degree of agreement here, one partner would always feel inhibited and the other would go through life feeling embarrassed.

Sharing

Someone who exhibits no sharing capability at all could be described as completely self-centered. Most of us probably aren't quite that bad and we try to be somewhat helpful and courteous to others while making sure we also look out for number one (ourselves). How much of our concern is for others versus how much is for ourselves differs, however. Mother Teresa would be an example of someone who is at the high end of the sharing scale, i.e. she has almost no self-centeredness. She takes nothing for herself, and gives her all to the poor of Calcutta. Nurses, social workers, people who volunteer for the Peace Corps, etc, might be considered high on the sharing scale. Others may think that it's each man/woman for himself/herself in this cruel world, and not feel much of a need to do anything for others. You don't need to make a value judgment here; simply recognize that a large difference on this criteria would be uncomfortable.

Culture

Being cultured is kind of a snobbish idea, but those who are cultured wouldn't have it any other way. This criteria could refer to your appreciation for fine art and literature, your taste in food, your preferences in clothing styles, the subjects you like to discuss, how important you think education is, whether you like opera or not. Some people really like classical music, and others don't. It would be quite possible to fake it for a while on this criteria, but I think that would be a mistake. Pretending to be someone you're not will eventually come back to bite you. If you hope to live with someone for a long time, you might as well let him/her know from the start what you're like. If beer and pizza is your idea of high class, find someone who agrees.

Honesty

Honest people can not tolerate crooks. Nor thieves, cheats, or liars. But none of us is totally saintly. So when you are looking for a mate, you want to look for someone who will cheat on income taxes only to the degree you would. Who would lie only when necessary, like you would. Be no more creative on the company expense report than you would be. How much fudging do you do on a loan application? Your job resume? Our society has brought us up to feel guilty for even minor transgressions with the truth, so we try to hide these things. But you can't hide them from your spouse. So you had better find a spouse with whom you feel comfortable on the honesty factor. You certainly don't want a spouse who is lower on the honesty scale than yourself. You need honesty to trust each other.

Family

Some people like to be closely involved with their immediate families, and/or and their extended family, sharing holidays together, perhaps living close to one another, etc. Some people will want to get advice and council from their parents, share their ups and downs with other family members, and have their kids grow up with their cousins. Other people might want to get out from under the influence of their families and would feel more comfortable being away from immediate family members. This could be a source of irritation if you and your mate have differing opinions about the closeness you want to have with your families.

Kids

The appropriate number of children to have seems to vary with the fashions of the time, and some people will want no children, some will want one or two kids, and some will want a large family. The biggest decision is whether to even have kids at all, because it would require a major concession for either partner to change his/her preference from zero kids to one, or from one to zero.

This is clearly a subject that has to be agreed upon in advance, because even one child changes everything. If you both agree to have kids, it is relatively easier to argue about whether to have two vs one, or three vs two. The tough decision is about the first one.

However, for your own benefit you may want to delay having kids, and for the kid's benefit, you'll probably be a better parent if you do. And for everybody's benefit, you want to pick the right mate so that the two of you raise them together.

Emotions: Calm or Passionate

Some people are very calm and not easily excited. Even if they are deeply in love you wouldn't be able to detect the attachment they feel for their partner. Their love may be true, but you probably wouldn't call it exciting. On the other end of the scale are the highly emotional people, tempestuous, wild, passionate. Their relationships are likely to be intense, stormy, and unpredictable.

Passion is like speed; it may be fun, but it doesn't come cheaply. If you buy a fast car for its high speed, you can't complain that it won't carry much luggage. If you want the thrill of a passionate mate, you will have to live with the instability that goes along with that kind of relationship.

Chauvinism: Decision making

In today's society, women are becoming educated more on a par with men, and more and more women have entered the work force. The issue of women's lib vs male chauvinism is a subject that can arouse heated debate, probably more so for the older generation who grew up when men were in charge of everything. But it's a subject that's not easily avoided when you have real chores that need to be done. How you decide to divide up the chores in a modern marriage will partially determine your compatibility on this criteria. If you and your mate both work, the decisions about who does what get even more difficult, and will be crucial to the happiness of your relationship. Working out an equitable sharing of duties and responsibilities is not easy, and the further apart you are on this scale, the harder it will be.

Obviously there is more to this category than just who does the household chores. Basically, this is a question about how decisions are made, and who really wears the pants in the family. It is probably one of those areas in the relationship that justifies the comments regarding having to work at a marriage. Like many of the other criteria, compatibility may not be easy to determine before you are actually married, but do your best.

Personality type: Child, Adult, Parent

An interesting book written a number of years ago explained that people approach interactions with other people from three different perspectives; from a childlike perspective, or from an adult perspective, or from a parent's perspective.

In *Transactional Analysis*, author Eric Berne says that in the "childlike" mode, a person is open, creative, inquisitive, uninhibited. This doesn't mean "childish", which has a negative connotation, but rather "childlike" which implies the way a child behaves before all the rules set in that confine our behavior. The author didn't include behaviors like star gazing, walking along the beach, or enjoying the sunset, but I would include these in this category, along with the more obvious childlike behaviors such as laughing, giggling, wrestling, etc.

In the "adult" mode, the person acts in a logical fashion, in an unemotional manner, dealing strictly with the facts. Being in this mode allows us to cope with the world and earn a living.

In the "parent" mode, a person is evaluative, critical, judgmental, and controlling. A real parent has to be in this mode at times with real children, but it is also possible to think and act from this perspective in any circumstance, even when among only adults.

Berne created these descriptions to explain why transactions between people either succeed or fail. A transaction between two people acting in the parent mode, criticizing something or everything, can carry on for some time. Two people in the adult mode can carry on forever, and this is how most work gets done and people exchange ideas. Two people can get a lot of fun out of both being in the child-like mode, wrestling around on the living room rug, just as if one or both of the people was actually a child.

A transaction also works if one person is in the parent mode and the other is in the child-like mode, taking direction or criticism. What doesn't work is a transaction where the lines cross, such as when one person is in the parent mode and the other person is trying to be factual and logical in the adult mode. Nor does it work when one person is in the adult mode trying to get something done and the other person is in the child mode being silly and not serious about the task at hand.

I think we can expand on his analysis and use it as a criteria on which to determine a more general compatibility between people. It was Berne's opinion that most people's personalities would have a fairly even distribution among these three modes, meaning that most of us bounce back and forth in our behavior and spend time in all three modes. However, there are people who do not have a good balance between these categories, and this could explain why you are uncomfortable spending an extended amount of time with them.

For example, some people seem to spend much of their time in the parent mode, and are always critical of somebody or something, and are always stating their opinion about how things ought to be. Others could be described as having too much adult and not enough child, and these people would be like a wet blanket when other people are able to let loose and have childlike, spontaneous, and carefree fun. On the other hand, some people may be in the childlike mode too much of the time, which can be fun, and perhaps generates a lot of creative output, but can be terribly frustrating to another person who is acting in the adult mode trying to deal with the reality of the real world.

Probably most people will have a reasonably balanced distribution of these three modes, but sometimes you find that you have a reaction to another person that you can't quite describe. I think that this is a useful model to help explain why some interactions are more comfortable than others, and why some relationships are more successful than others. If you find it helpful, use it in your own selection process.

Sociability

By this I mean someone's attitude about being in the company of other people. Some people like to entertain, and go to parties, etc., but others don't. Some people can't stand to be alone for more than short periods of time, and will try to find someone to be around, someone to do things with. Others are perfectly content to spend extended periods of time all by themselves, and may actually prefer not to have anybody around. I suggest that you pick your own position on this scale, and try to find someone who is compatible.

Religion

With regard to religion, or spirituality in general, there are two aspects to consider. One is what you believe, the other is how strongly you believe it. Whether you believe in one of the conventional American religions, or Islam, or Buddhism, or a new religion of ecology, a very strong belief will have an effect on your behavior. A strong belief system usually means behaving in a very prescribed way and giving up something in pursuit of some higher goal. The history of the world includes a lot of wars over this subject, and people can still get very heated up with others who have opposing points of view. I don't think people want to compromise much on this criteria, so it's probably best that you look for someone who believes the way you do. Keep in mind that, even if the two of you are exceptionally open minded and are able to make an unusual relationship work, your relatives may have difficulty accepting the relationship.

Ambition

Ambition is an inner drive to accomplish something. It can't be transferred to anyone else, and you can't train somebody to have it. I don't know exactly what it is, but I know some of us have more of it than others. The pursuit of any goal requires some trade-offs and some sacrifices, and someone with lesser ambition may not be willing to make those sacrifices. Politics is a good example that we can all visualize. Anyone with an ambition in politics had better have a spouse who agrees that the goal is worth working that hard for and is willing to be a supportive helpmate. Imagine living with someone who is striving to be an Olympic athlete.

Wealth and power are things that people strive for. Others strive to be the very best at something, whether it be in music, or sports, or business, or whatever. Not everyone is willing to work that hard, though, and most of us are satisfied with a more modest level of accomplishment. If there is too much difference on this scale, the more ambitious of the pair will feel that the other is holding him/her back on the way to success. And the other will feel that too much is being given up in the pursuit of just that one goal.

Ambition is usually discussed in relation to one's career, and it usually implies that in order to be successful and earn a good income, you will have to work hard at it. This means nights at the office, trips out of town, perhaps delaying family plans because something important came up. If both of you work and the woman is pursuing her own career, this can get quite complicated.

It would be wise to think about what your goals in life are, and compare these to those of your potential mate. What do you do when baby comes along? Who changes career goals to take care of the little rascal? What are your priorities regarding work vs family?

Some authors view ambition as a desirable characteristic that for sure you want your mate to have. I disagree. Ambition reminds me of the bodybuilder's motto of "No pain: No gain". Nothing comes for free and some people may not want to pay the price. I think that it is up to you to decide what level of ambition you are comfortable with, and then find someone with a compatible philosophy.

Looks

Some people are concerned that men place too much emphasis on this criteria. They think that men search for only the best looking women and pass up many good, but less attractive, women in the process. Evolutionary biology provides an explanation for this. It says that a woman's appearance was an indicator of her healthiness, and dominant males would prefer to mate with women who were healthy because healthy females would be better able to raise children who would survive. Which appearance factors (i.e.

indicators of healthiness) are considered attractive, however, is open to debate. Looking at pictures in the history books and National Geographic would lead one to believe that those factors have changed throughout history and they vary across the different cultures.

There is no doubt that both men and women are attracted by good looks, and the media certainly places much emphasis on them! It may be that we are not as overly focused on looks as we would think however. One survey indicated that only 40% of men thought that looks were an important requirement in a mate. If that is even close to true, people who fall below the expected standard of "beautiful" should simply work to keep themselves presentable and focus on other attributes which will be attractive to potential mates.

As I look about me in my community and among my friends and associates, I see a lot of happily married people who are not necessarily very attractive. Studies have shown that attractive people may see more action in the dating scene, but it is the more average people who do better at finding a mate. The conclusion I have come to is that looks is one of the criteria that can be most easily compromised. Fortunately, we all seem to have differing opinions about who is attractive and who isn't, so go for the best looking one you can find who meets your other criteria.

Status

This criteria is a corollary to the previous one, and also has an explanation based on evolutionary biology. Throughout human history, women have tried to pair up with high status males who were capable of providing them with resources. Life was physically very difficult, and it made good evolutionary sense to attract a man who could provide for the family and the rearing of children. However, even though our circumstances have changed dramatically, for many women the pursuit of a dominant male is still a central theme in their search for a mate. This may be causing more anxiety than necessary.

This issue is complicated in our modern society because we humans are such a complex species that it is no longer clear what criteria should be used in trying to determine who is dominant in this context. In the animal world, size and strength are obviously critical characteristics of the dominant male, but these don't mean so much to our human species because we also depend on other factors such as intelligence and cooperative effort. In fact, the criteria required for dominance have become more numerous, and we need to put all this into its proper perspective.

Status, or social standing, in our society is getting more difficult to define all the time. It used to be quite simple. If you were born into the royal family, you were a prince or princess, pure and simple. It didn't matter how ugly you were, or how dumb, you were still a member of the royal family, and as such, had the highest possible status.

During the industrial revolution, which started about two hundred years ago, certain families amassed tremendous fortunes and gained control of enormous amounts of land and property. Members of those families were considered to have had very high status. They weren't royalty, but they had money.

As society developed further, government got bigger and more powerful, and there were families that rose to the top of the political hierarchy. Even though they perhaps didn't have either money or royalty, they had high status because of their power.

Eventually, companies got so big that they were no longer controlled by the family owners, and a class of professional managers arose. Those who controlled large companies gained high status, based on the importance of their jobs.

As we move into the present, we find that the best people in the arts can now also obtain high status, because modern travel and communications will permit large audiences to approve of their work. Writers and scholars can obtain high status, based on the worldwide acceptance of their ideas and the skill of their writing. In fact, in our modern society, status can be obtained in many ways. In short, status isn't what it used to be; it's spread around too much.

Status is still an issue, however, and there are still status factors that contribute to your overall social standing. These factors would include the status of your family, your education, type of job, level of position, income, command of the language, and perhaps a few other things. Status may have been diluted to the point where it doesn't have the impact it once did, but we still all have some vague notions about status. Marrying up the scale would be great, but what will you do to deserve it?

A second factor has to be added when it comes to searching for a high status male in our modern society, and that is a man's willingness to stick around and be the father. In earlier times and in other cultures, a high status successful male who wanted another female could acquire a second mate without having to give up the first one. The first female might lose some of his resources because of the second female, but she would not lose all of them. In a monogamous society like ours, however, we don't let the male have the second female unless he gives up the first one.

Even though we have instituted the concept of alimony as a partial remedy for this, it does not make up for the fact that the kids from the first mate have lost their father. How many women want to go to the effort of capturing a high status male if he later runs off with another female? Clearly, under these new conditions, the likelihood of a man staying with his marriage is just as important a factor in selecting a man as his status.

Individuality: Other-Directed vs Inner-Directed

People who are inner-directed are driven by some internal motivation that causes them to do what they feel should be done, no matter what anybody else thinks or does. Inner-directed people try to satisfy their own standards. An inner directed person keeps the house clean because he/she wants it that way.

Other-directed means that your behavior is affected by what other people may think or do. Other-directed people are very conscious of what's in style, what's popular, what's politically correct, and try to "keep up with the Jones". The other-directed person cleans the house because company is coming. Your position on this scale will determine how you dress, what kind of a car you drive, even what college you think your kids ought to go to.

This criteria will also determine whether you select a mate who satisfies your own needs, or whether you select someone who satisfies everybody else's idea of an acceptable mate. I strongly urge you to read the book *How to Stop Looking For Someone Perfect And Find Someone To Love*, by Dr. Judith Sills. She does an excellent job of describing how to avoid the search for the wrong mate so you can concentrate on searching for the mate who will truly make you happy. I think, however, that only the inner-directed people will be interested in taking advantage of her advice.

Dominance

You have to be very careful to distinguish between dominance and abuse. Usually it is the man who is the abuser, and abusive men come from all racial, ethnic, religious, and socioeconomic groups in society. They fall into different categories of abusive behavior, but the one thing they all have in common is the need to control.

You must terminate the relationship immediately if you are abused and you're not even married yet. This is a book about planning, so make yourself a vow here and now that you will never be beaten up the second time.

Some people, even without being abusive, have a very strong need to be in charge. They need to dominate, make the decisions, tell others what to do. At the other end of this scale are those who are willing to follow, who are indecisive, who like to take direction, who like to be taken care of. Perhaps in the middle of this scale are those who believe in the live-and-let-live philosophy. They don't want anybody to tell them what to do, but neither do they have the need to tell anybody else what to do. You need to figure out what kind of a person you are comfortable with on this criteria.

Energy Level

Have you ever watched someone who works, works, works and never gets tired? Some of us wouldn't last long if we were married to one of those types. And there are others who manage to lounge around all the time and never get anything done at all. They think the task isn't that important anyway, so they'll get to it tomorrow.

If you and your potential mate were to go on a hypothetical vacation, how would you spend your time? Would you be willing to sit on the beach and read, or would you have every minute of the day scheduled out for sight seeing? There really is no right or wrong position on this scale; we're all just built differently. Be selective, though, because most of us have developed a comfortable pace and would have a hard time accommodating someone who is too different from ourselves.

Intelligence

Since intelligence is a quality where more is better, it would seem wise to try to attract the smartest person you can. I would agree with this, with one word of caution. If the other person is the smarter, then you are the dumber, and if you are too much dumber, the other party might eventually lose interest in you. So go for somebody smart, but with the understanding that to make the match work, you may have to be open minded and willing to learn in order to keep up.

Sex

Suffice it to say that individuals will differ considerably on what they think about sex, what preferences they have, how often they like sex, and so forth. Just as with all the other criteria, you will surely be much happier if you find someone with whom you are compatible.

I have a big word of caution here, though. Good sex is most probably one of your objectives in marriage as well as being a criteria by which to select a mate. But I am convinced that good sex requires compatibility on all the other criteria as well as on this one. At one end of the spectrum is the couple that is blissfully happy, who will probably have a good sex life. However, a couple that is on the verge of divorce will probably have no sex, which establishes the other end of the spectrum.

Even if you start out with good sex and then you find that you're not compatible on some other issues, and you fight a lot, where do you think you'll end up on this sex scale? Because sex is such an important subject, but is too complicated to be covered adequately in this section, a more extensive discussion on sex is presented in the next chapter.

Risk-Taking

Risk-taking varies from being very cautious to being very bold and daring. Normally, risk is associated with gambling, which is the easiest example to think of, or playing the stock market perhaps. But there are lots of areas in life where this factor comes into play. If you have lived in one place all your life, you might be reluctant to move to another city, because of the uncertainty (risk) of how the move might turn out. Some people, however, may have moved so much they wouldn't see changing cities as much of a risk. Your attitude toward risk will show up in how you buy insurance. Changing jobs involves risk, so does driving fast. You might agree with the one type of risk but not the other. Leaving a steady job to go into business for yourself involves risk, and some spouses would approve of it and some wouldn't. How about being married to someone in a high risk occupation?

How about taking a job in some foreign country? How about flying when the weather is bad? If two people don't pretty much agree on the risk issue, and have a similar comfort zone, one is going to be a nervous wreck watching the behavior of the other.

Communication

Some people hardly talk at all, and others seem to talk all the time. There are those who insist on talking even though they have nothing to say, and there are those whom you wish would express themselves more than they do. Some people are enjoyable to talk with, and are good listeners. Others are argumentative, and always insist on telling you how wrong all of your opinions are. Perhaps as important as the quantity of talk is the level to which personal feelings are expressed. Some people feel the need to share their hopes, sorrows, and fears, and want to hear about yours. Others feel this is too personal and don't enjoy conversations of this type.

My father gave me a story that illustrates the quiet type. In the story the wife complains to her taciturn husband that he never says he loves her. To which the husband replies "I told you that I loved you when I married you, and I'll let you know if I ever change my mind."

Communication is a very difficult subject, and it could take you a long time to decide whether you're compatible with another person on this criteria. You probably hear more about "poor communication" being the reason for failure in marriage than any other. One explanation is that men and women talk for different reasons: women talk for rapport, whereas men talk for information. How you react to stress and disagreements could be quite different, and you may wonder if you could ever learn to get along together. This can be a major problem even for couples who are well matched, simply because men and women are very different in this regard.

Don't discard a potentially good mate because you think he/she doesn't communicate well with you. Read the book *You Just Don't Understand: Women and Men in*

Conversation by Deborah Tannen. This is a difference that can be improved upon. Learn more about what this all means so you and your mate can overcome this typical problem.

Organization

Do you know anyone who can never find his/her car keys? Does that bother you? If so, you'd better look for someone who is as organized as you are. Do you insist that birthday cards get mailed out on time? Or do you get them sent whenever you remember to do it? Do you get a haircut whenever you can find time, or do you get one every third Thursday at 4:30 from the same barber? Do you care whether your shoes are freshly polished or not? Do you take time out to get your oil changed every 5000 miles, plus or minus 100? Do you allow "stuff" to accumulate in your car, or do you clean it out every time? Does your yard have a few weeds, or have you picked every last one of those little suckers out of there? Do you pay your bills on time and keep a balanced checkbook? Some of us might not think this is a very serious criteria, but I'm sure that some others will.

Diligence

Diligence means that you persevere in working toward a goal that you set. Some people work on painting the house until it's finished, others may take a few months to get the job done. If you need to lose weight, do you keep at it until you succeed? If you start a project, do you finish it? Some people feel comfortable about changing goals and switching projects; others are compulsive about staying with a task until it is complete. Diligence may not seem like an important criteria unless the goal is significant, such as saving money or completing a degree, but it's worth thinking about.

Lifestyle: rural or urban

For lack of a better way to summarize this, I will refer to this as a big city vs small town mentality, although it is really more complicated than that. Having lived in both, I think there is a difference between how city people view the world versus how country people view the world, and the expectations they have for their environment differ. My country friends wonder how anyone can live in an environment that is so smoggy, so full of traffic, so full of people that you can't possibly know most of the people around you. My city friends, on the other hand, wonder how country folk can live in an area without 24 hour supermarkets, without an airport close by, and with only one movie theater that shows two movies a week.

The differences go deeper than that, of course. Depending on your family and background, you will have your own personal expectations about things like individual freedoms, obligations to neighbors, the need for space, the use of time, the degree of automation required for a comfortable life. Families differ in their priorities of what is considered important, and can define success differently, and you will have grown up with those values.

These are such a part of you that you don't think much about them, but they will become painfully obvious if you deal with someone whose view of life differs dramatically from yours. Even the best matched couples will find something to argue about now and then, but hopefully the subject will be inconsequential and the conflict brief. Disagreements about important personal characteristics can't be resolved so easily, however, and these characteristics need to be considered in your selection process.

The forgoing list of criteria describes some of the areas that I think are important in determining whether or not two people can be compatible with each other in the long run. Use this list as a starting point and devise a list of your own.

Let me state again the premise of this book. It is my belief that unhappiness in marriage occurs when there is a mismatch on several or more of your criteria for compatibility. Unless you are an unusually tolerant person, each little mismatch bugs you now and then, and the more of them there are, the more chances of your being irritated. The larger the mismatch, the more severe the discomfort. You may have a high level of tolerance for this sort of a problem, but at some point, if the differences get too numerous or too severe, it becomes intolerable. So, if you don't want to end up in an unhappy marriage, or a divorce, select a mate with whom you have minimum differences. This is the essence of my theory on compatibility.

6

SEX

Sex is not only one of the criteria by which you select a mate, it is also one of the primary reasons for even having a mate. Because sex can no longer be taken for granted, sex has to be an important entry on your list of criteria for selecting a mate. Why would you want a mate if having the mate didn't fulfill your requirements for a satisfactory sex life? The answer to this fundamental question may depend on whether you are a man or a woman, and that is precisely the problem I want to address.

The changes in our society and the world over the last twenty or thirty years have had a profound effect on the issue of sex in marriage. (And sex before marriage, as well). The roles of men and women in the workplace and in society are much different today than they were in the past, and these changes have had a dramatic effect on the subject of sex. In my opinion the changes in our society have occurred faster than our ability to cope with them, and there will be a lot of confusion until some new attitudes and behaviors are agreed upon and accepted.

Fifty years ago, virginity until marriage was very common, at least in the public perception. Most churches of the day recommended abstinence until marriage, and the Catholic Church, among others, took a pretty strong stance against premarital sex. Those who did engage in sex outside marriage knew it was wrong and were taught to feel guilty about it afterwards. In those days, females who had a liberal attitude towards sex put their reputations at risk. At best they were referred to as loose women; at worst they were called tramps, or sluts, or some equally negative equivalent. But of course the boys wanted to date these girls because the boys wanted to have the sex.

Prior to 1950, because sex was socially acceptable only when associated with marriage, most couples in a normal dating scenario at that time postponed sex until after marriage, or at least until the couple was dating seriously. Marriage was very common by the age 18 or 20, which was not surprising, since the urge for sex is so strong at that age. Early marriage was especially true among those who did not go to college. On the other hand, if a person got to be as old as, say 30, and wasn't married yet, people would start wondering what the problem was.

In my opinion, whether done consciously or unconsciously, this pattern of sex that existed in the past can be characterized as a trade off, or a quid pro quo, or an exchange of one valuable thing for another. I wish I knew whom to give credit for this expression, which says very succinctly what used to be the tradeoff:

> Marriage is the price men pay for sex.
> Sex is the price women pay for marriage.

Because society sort of pressured a person into marriage in order to get sex, society had to support sex if it occurred within the marriage, and it did. Although it was never stated directly as far as I know, I always had the feeling that the "rules" were designed to protect the woman before marriage, and to protect the man after marriage. I had a Catholic roommate once who informed me that the church's position on sex was that, within marriage, you never said no to a request for sex from your partner. Although the "rule" did not specifically cater to either gender, it was clear to me that in most cases the rule was intended to support the man's desire for sex. Except for during her period, and the occasional "I have a headache tonite", the woman was expected to comply with the man's request for sex. Although the other mainline churches may not have had such an explicit guideline on sexual obligations, the same philosophy was pretty much accepted throughout society.

Sex in The 60's, 70's and 80's

Our attitudes towards sex loosened up considerably in the 60's, and this was a wonderful period in history for a man to be a bachelor. Bachelors could have lots of sex without having to pay the price of marriage to get it. But single women had a good time also, being liberated enough to pursue their own potential in the areas of work, leisure, self development, and sex as well, if they chose to.

Sex in The 90's

Nothing comes without a price, though, and the price has been very high. Social diseases are so prevalent that anyone who now has unprotected sex is crazy. In my day, gonorrhea and syphilis were the "social diseases" to worry about, and they are still with us. But since then, others have been added to the list, including herpes, chlamydia, and now AIDS. One of them is bound to get you unless you practice safe sex, or even better, a combination of safe sex and contraception.

What had become almost a free-sex society has had to become much more restricted again. We're back to an era when you can't trust that your sex will be safe just because your partner is a 'nice' person. Anyone could have one of these STD's (sexually transmitted diseases), and the only way to protect yourself is to behave as though everyone does. Syphilis, gonorrhea and chlamydia can be treated, but are serious if not caught early. Herpes you can't get rid of. AIDS will just kill you. Safe sex is the only smart way to go anymore, until you are absolutely sure of your partner. You deserve no sympathy if you don't practice safe sex.

This concern for safety is bound to have an effect on how people treat sex during the dating process, which unfortunately will also complicate the issue of sex during marriage as well. You need to know that you and your potential mate have compatible ideas and behaviors regarding sex, because your life together will not be satisfactory if you aren't compatible. Sex preferences that are immediately obvious can be discovered during the dating process, but what you need to be concerned with is what happens to your sex life after years of marriage. Men and women are built differently, and may develop diverging attitudes about sex after years of living with the same sex partner, especially if there are children.

Because sex is still a subject that many people are uncomfortable discussing, it is not easy to find out what people really do or think regarding sex. There have been lots of little surveys reported in various magazines, but they are too limited in scope and too small in sample size to be helpful in understanding the full subject. Some years ago the only large scale studies about sex were the Kinsey Report and the work done by Masters and Johnson, but they didn't provide all the answers we need to know when it comes to marriage. So, where can one find some valid and useful information? I've done a lot of reading, and I can assure you that it's not easy. It has taken me a long time to write this chapter.

One of the places I have found helpful in looking for information on what people think about sex is in the columns written by Dear Abby, Ann Landers, and Dr. Joyce Brothers. They each have such a long history of talking to so many people that they have a pretty good perspective on a number of different subjects. Every now and then there is a letter about sex in one of their columns, and some of these letters can be very informative. Individual opinions usually can't be generalized, but if you read enough of these letters, you begin to get the picture. Consider these letters to Ann Landers with opposing points of view from one of her columns in the Los Angeles Times, under the heading: Sex is a Turnoff for Many Women:

> DEAR ANN: You really blew your response to "Fouled and Furious in Tennessee." The wife, married 40 years and the mother of five, wrote about her "horny old goat." She was in good health but no longer interested in sex. Your response made it sound as if something were wrong with her. You suggested that she get professional help, as if she were mentally ill or something.
>
> If you didn't get a zillion complaints for that answer, you should have. I'll bet a lot of women who read your column are also plain fed up with sex. If you want a poll that will knock your socks off, ask your female readers: "How many of you would be happy not to have to bother with it again?" I'll bet you wouldn't have the nerve to print the results.
> -St. Petersburg

DEAR ST. PETE: In 1984, I did the poll you suggested, and the results didn't surprise me in the least. They were exactly what I expected. You can't write a column like mine for 37 years and not learn something. On Nov 4, 1984, I asked the following question: "Would you be content to be held close and treated tenderly and forget about "the act"? Reply YES of NO and add one line: 'I am over (or under) 40 years of age'. No signature is necessary."

A few weeks later, I reported to my readers that I had received more than 90,000 responses. I told them: "The mail room looks like a disaster area. We have put on extra help. The employees are working double shifts and weekends, yet the mailbags seem to multiply like rabbits."

Was I surprised at the outcome? No. I could have guessed the way it would go. But I never dreamed that more than 90,000 women would be moved to express themselves on such an intimate subject. Nor would I have predicted the percentages or the passion with which so many women described their sex lives. The greatest revelation, however, is what the poll says about men as lovers. Clearly, there is trouble in paradise.

The poll revealed that 72% of the respondents said they would be content to be held close and treated tenderly and forget about "the act." A full 40% of those wanting to forget about "the act" were under 40 years old. That was the most surprising aspect of the survey.

Many of the 28% who voted "no" said they needed the sexual climax to relieve physical tension. Almost as many said they need the ultimate in gratification, and anything less would make them feel exploited and used.

A woman in Anchorage wrote: " I am 26 and want three children, so obviously I need more than conversation. After I have my family, I'd gladly settle for separate bedrooms. Sex doesn't do a thing for me."

FROM KANSAS CITY; I'm 55 and vote "yes." Cuddling is the best part. My first husband was insensitive and uncaring. He used to practically rape me five times a week. If a date had treated me like that, I would have had him arrested.

TEXARKANA: I hate sex. I was relieved when my husband died. My present husband is on heart pills and is impotent. It's heaven to be held and cuddled.

Not all the respondents had these reactions. Remember, 28% had the opposite attitude. The only one quoted in that particular article said:

EUREKA, CALIF.: I vote "no." If my old man were over the hill, I'd settle for high school necking, but as long as he's able to shake the walls and wake up the downstairs neighbors, I want to get in on the action.

As with all samples, we have to be careful with the statistics quoted, because they may not represent the population at large. However, 90,000 is a very, very large sample, which lends it a lot of credibility. Among the readers of Ann Landers, at least, women who don't like sex will be delighted to hear that their opinion is held in common with 72% of their peers. On the other hand, men will be appalled to learn that 3 out of 4 of these women don't even want sex.

In a subsequent column a few days later, on older woman wrote in to say that her two male friends were both impotent, and if there were any women out there who were being bothered by men's advances, she would be happy to have those men sent over to "bother" her.

You can see that what we have here is the basis for some very heated discussion and some very unhappy marriages. Since the reader is presumably still single and is not yet caught in this dilemma, I would suggest some serious thought about this as a criteria for selecting a mate.

The first thing to do is to acknowledge that men and women are built differently. For those readers who want to delve more deeply into the origins of human sexuality, the explanations provided by evolutionary psychologists give us a fascinating insight into why we behave as we do. Robert Wright's book *The Moral Animal: Evolutionary Psychology and Everyday Life* explains mate selection in many of the animal species, including the ape species which are most like us, in addition to analyzing our own past and present human behavior. He discusses monogamy, adultery, fidelity, jealousy, and how we developed many of the behaviors that might now be called "natural". He also says that we may have to inhibit some of these impulses for the sake of marriage in our modern society.

The theory of evolution suggests that the males who get more of their genes into the gene pool will be more likely to have their offspring make it into the next generation, so evolution favors sexually active males. The human species may have developed intellectually over the last few centuries to the point where our sexual behavior is socially modified, but not enough time has elapsed to modify us physiologically. Men are still built with an internal mechanism that drives them toward the completion of sex. Otherwise, what would drive the species to try to reproduce itself?

Like everything else, how much interest one has in sex will have a distribution throughout the population, and some will like it more than others. Some females will only enjoy sex until they have had the children they want, and then, as the survey indicates, they have a much reduced desire for further sex. Although many women do like sex, some of them into old age, it is not as necessary that they enjoy it as it is for men. There is no physiological reason why females have to like sex, because women can get pregnant and propagate the species without ever having to get any pleasure from sex. All they have to do is to submit, because the males will supply all the desire that is required. Once the female has had her babies, or gets too old to be a mother any more, there is even less of a direct biological need for the female to continue to have sex.

Whether women should or shouldn't enjoy sex can be argued, but if the survey described by Ann Landers is even close to representative, the fact is that many don't. While there may be a distribution among the female population regarding how much interest they have in sex, both before and after having babies, it appears that a large portion in fact don't want to have sex.

Males don't have the same biological events such as childbirth and menopause to indicate that their time is up and sex is no longer a biological imperative. Men are built to try to sow their seeds as much as possible for as long as possible. This desire for sex will have a distribution across the male population, as it does for the females, but the foregoing reasoning would indicate that there are not very many men at the end of the scale that is labeled "no interest in sex".

This has been substantiated dramatically in a follow-up survey which Ann Landers made in late 1995, and her results provide a pretty good indication of how men feel about sex. This time she asked the men whether they would be willing to forget about the act and settle for being held tenderly. Of 67,000 responses, only 5,600 men would be willing to do that, and most of those were over 60 years old. The majority, 92%, said no, they want sex.

Margaret Kent, in her book, *How To Marry The Man Of Your Choice*, says that "sex is a predominant thought in the mind of a normal man, second only to self preservation. If a man does not have to worry about his survival, he thinks about satisfying his sexual needs." You can see that we have a big problem here. In contrast to the men, females will engage in sex during courtship and until they get the children they desire, but the Ann Landers survey implies that after that, 3 out of 4 women would just as soon quit with the sex program.

If all of this data and analysis is correct, what this means is that we have two distributions that don't match very well.

What needs to be considered here is the big picture. Humans are a species that requires a high male-parent investment, which means that it is important that the men contribute to the rearing of the children. If women want to provide the best possible environment for their children, they need to have the men stick around and help. Marriage is the institution through which fathers provide that help, but the marriage has to be attractive enough to keep the fathers involved in it.

From the men's point of view, the problem is that there is no longer the tradeoff that used to exist, i.e. marriage in return for sex. Women's lib has allowed women in our modern society to be their own persons, and if that means that they don't want to have sex, they don't have to have sex. When a woman has a job and contributes to the family's income, she doesn't feel quite as dependent on the male as in earlier times. And even if she doesn't work, there is now the attitude that she can't be forced to do something she doesn't want to do. Husbands can even be convicted of raping their wives, which was unheard of twenty or thirty years ago. Why should the man remain in a marriage, keeping his end of the bargain, if the wife doesn't keep her end of the bargain by providing sex?

Naturally, there have to be cases where the situation is reversed. There are lots of articles and books about men who have a physical disability or some psychological hang-up and have a problem with sex, but these typically describe individual cases and don't necessarily relate to men in general. And there are surveys, of course, that show there are women who want more sex. Reader polls in some women's magazines, for instance, indicate a high interest in sex, and women are quoted as saying that they would like more sex than they are currently getting. These surveys provide an interesting contrast to the findings of Ann Lander's study, but they are not carefully controlled, and therefore do not necessarily represent the population at large.

One recent study that I am aware of that has been presented as accurately representing the population at large was in the *Family Planning Perspectives*, the journal of the Alan Guttmacher Institute. It states that in a study of 3,321 men ages 20-39, some have a good sex life, but the mean frequency for sex is about once a week. This may or may not be comforting news to those who are already married, depending on whether this supports their own behavior or not. What is not discussed by the reviewers of this data, but is of great significance to the readers of this book, is the effect of this information on future marriages. Are you (men) willing to go through all the trials and tribulations of marriage in return for sex once a week? Or less than once a week, which is what happens to half the married men in this study?

Since the men in this study are young men, ages 20-39, age is probably not a factor in the low sexual frequency reported by half the group. There are three other possible explanations that seem most probable to me. First, it is possible that the wives just don't want any more sex than that, so the men have to settle for less sex than they would really like. Second, their lives may be so hectic that they don't have the time or energy for an adequate sex life. Or, third, perhaps their relationships have deteriorated to the point where both the spouses are unhappy with each other and there is not much desire for sex between them.

Whichever it is, this is not the kind of news a man wants to hear when he is deciding whether or not to get married and have children. The same study said that for single men the mean frequency for sex is also once a week, so what's the benefit of getting married if you can get as much sex while staying single? It appears that marriage will have to offer something other than sex, or half of the men will be sadly disappointed.

Another study, *The National Health and Social Life Survey*, which has been published by the University of Chicago Press as a book titled *Sex In America: A Definitive Survey* obtained similar results from a sample of 3,432 people aged 18 to 59. Of the married people questioned, about 40% have sex twice a week or more, but the rest have sex several times a month or less. They report that sexual frequency peaks with the 25-29 year old age group and then declines with age. (And perhaps as a function of having been married longer, but they did not include the data to support that.) This study also showed that those living together have more sex than married people.

What Margaret Kent suggests is that the woman ascertain the man's natural sex cycle and see if she wants to meet it. Putting the man off until he gets argumentative and grouchy will determine the minimum limit of his cycle, and increasing the frequency until he cries ouch will determine the maximum limit of his cycle. The woman can then adjust to some frequency within that range.

Most likely any major mismatch will be discovered prior to marriage, but not necessarily. The remaining problem is that your preferred frequency, or your partner's, may change with time, as discussed above. What I would propose (only half kidding) is that there must be some kind of a law of limitations that says a woman can have kids, a career, or a sex life, pick any two. I don't know how to solve this problem. All I can do is alert you to it so you can try to find your own solution.

Somewhere in our human evolution, human females learned that they could also get enjoyment from sex. Dr. Irene Kassorda says, in *Nice Girls Do*, that there are legends about female sexuality dating back to the Neolithic period which suggest that it was women, not men, who were considered more active sexually. Her explanation is that our current problems with sex may have started when men decided that female sensuality had to be contained and controlled so that paternity issues could be established, which then allowed the development of laws regarding property and inheritance. She explains how Freud and his predecessors had a further negative impact on female sexuality, and how we are still suffering from their influence on our thinking. *Nice Girls Do* was one of the earlier books about how to overcome that influence by taking a positive attitude toward sex, and was a best seller. There are now numerous books and articles in the women's magazines on this topic, all trying to help women learn to get more enjoyment from sex.

Part of the explanation may be attributed to men's failure to provide for the emotional needs of women, which makes it difficult for them to respond sexually. Ellen Kreidman, in an article in *Family Circle*, explains that men and women are different, based on her experiences in the relationship classes she teaches. She says that when asked what their mates do to make them feel loved or content, men refer to having their physical needs met, whereas women refer to having their emotional needs met.

She gets very different responses when she asks the meaning of sensuality. The men describe sexually explicit encounters with one or more naked women. You might say they picture x-rated scenes, she says. The women describe romantic encounters, such as a couple dancing close together, holding hands on a moonlit beach, or gazing into each others eyes over a candlelight dinner. Their images are PG.

A man gets excited by visual images; pictures of women in alluring outfits, negligees, erotic poses, etc. A woman gets more excited by words, which is why so many women read romance novels.

Her conclusion after a decade of observing and teaching men and women: most women don't truly understand how strong a man's sex drive really is, and most men don't have a clue how emotionally starved most women are.

A woman who enjoys sex and is an active partner doubles the pleasure that a man derives from sex. Every man wants to feel wanted and needed physically, and they want their mates to be responsive. The ultimate turn-on for a man is when she's turned on.

However, she says, if a woman is not getting her emotional needs met, it is almost impossible for her to respond sexually. For women, kindness, gentleness, devotion, commitment, attention, patience and compliments are sexy. She says that a woman's desire for sex results from feeling cared for, cherished and loved. A woman whose mate takes the time to let her know that she's special, needed, appreciated, and loved will be far more available sexually than a woman who is neglected or ignored.

Further complicating the discussion is a book by Helen Fisher, called *Anatomy of Love, The Natural History of Monogamy, Adultery, and Divorce*. She says that romance developed as part of the evolutionary process in order to keep a male and female together in a long term partnership, which was essential for child rearing. The mutual attraction apparently declines in about four years however, and divorce rates peak at about the fourth year in most of the 62 cultures she studied. If there is a second child three years later, this might prolong the attraction, which would then give rise to the "seven year itch" made famous by Marilyn Monroe in a movie by that name. Whether it's four years or seven, apparently nature provides for a mutual attraction for only so long, and it will take some special efforts to keep the relationship together after that.

I think you can see from the length and complexity of this discussion that it will be difficult for both men and women to determine what their own sexual frequency will be after some years of marriage. In an era when women are allowed to say no if they don't want to have sex, it is more likely that the men will now be doing the suffering if there is a mismatch on this criteria.

Or, they will find an alternative. One man responding to Ann Lander's survey said that the lack of sex at home is why we have massage parlors, dating services, call girls, topless bars and prostitution. Others said that they found their solution to the problem by having a relationship with another woman.

Or a third alternative. According to the survey in *Sex In America*, a majority of the men and almost half of the women augment their partnered sex with solo sex. In the future there are likely to be high tech alternatives which will be appealing to some and appalling to others. Sexual simulators are not well described yet, but could be something like a complex body stocking, with moving actuators, in a virtual reality environment. This will not happen for a few years yet, so it is too early to get any particulars, but I have no doubt that this is technically feasible and that it will happen.

One way to look at these alternatives is that it could take the burden off the partner who is not interested in sex. The other way of viewing it is that it could eliminate the need for that partner. The obvious conclusion is that it is still important that you be sexually compatible with your mate.

Men: It appears that you can no longer count on getting sex just by virtue of being married. You are going to have to earn it by treating your lady nicely and with respect.

Ladies: Above the age of thirty, there are fewer men than women, and the shortage of men gets worse as you go up in age. A lack of interest in sex means you will have to work even harder at finding a mate, and then trying to keep him. You will have a much better chance for a happy marriage if you are in the 28% that enjoy sex, which is what most men are looking for.

7

THE SEARCH

In many societies around the world, at least historically, your parents picked your mate for you. In our society you, yourself, have to make it happen, and most of us prefer it that way. But, Prince Charming or Princess Charming is not going to come knocking on your door, and you're going to have to take action yourself if you want to find the perfect mate.

I hope that I have convinced you that you really are, and should be, particular about whom you select for a mate, and that finding that special person is going to be somewhat difficult. To improve your effectiveness in the search for a mate, I suggest that you think of yourself as a salesman. You are trying to sell a product (you) that could be of interest to as many as one quarter of the U.S. population. Think of the salespeople you know who sell a product that almost everybody might want to buy. Examples: real estate, life insurance, Amway, Tupperware, etc. Do you think these salespeople are ever off guard when it comes to a potential sales opportunity? Never. Not the good ones, anyway. All of these salespeople have to keep plugging away, keeping their eyes open looking for new prospects, and so do you.

Let's review the numbers. If you decide that there are ten criteria that are important to you, and half the people you meet qualify on any one of those criteria, it will take a thousand candidates to find the person who qualifies on all ten. For twenty criteria, it will take a million.

What can you do if the chances of finding a mate are so slim? What I think happens too often is that people overlook or ignore some of the important criteria for compatibility and settle for a mate with less than perfect compatibility. Even more likely, they think that they can change the other person. This almost never works, which is why we have so much unhappiness in marriage.

I think the better choice is to increase the number of candidates in order to make it more likely that you find one you really want. This is not going to happen easily, so you need a plan. I'm sure that you have heard all the standard advice about the fact that you have to get out and about. Mr./Mrs. Right is not going to find you if you are at home watching television. But I have two suggestions. First, only get involved in activities that are of real interest to you, so you don't feel disappointed if the activity doesn't lead immediately to finding a mate. Second, look for people whom you would like to date, not for people whom you want to marry. If you are so desperate for a mate that you impose all your criteria too soon, before a relationship even starts, you will filter everybody out. Accept the fact that you are going to be single for a while, and figure out how to cope with life and enjoy yourself in the meantime while you continue to search.

Many people say they are too busy to have time to even date, much less look for the perfect mate. Their work is a full time obsession, or they are single parents who are totally occupied with family matters during the hours that would otherwise be available for dating. There is no question that today's lifestyles are hectic, but that means you just have to be more clever about working it into your schedule.

Consider yourself always on duty. Every person with whom you come in contact should be considered a candidate, and sometimes you will have to initiate the contact. Most of us are fairly reluctant to do these things, but maybe you can develop this skill. Read *50 Ways To Find A Lover* by Sharyn Wolf for some very good suggestions on how to meet people.

My advice is to try to think like a salesman, even if you can't bring yourself to behave like one. As a salesman, my thinking would go like this: no matter where you are, if you are not exceptionally good looking, the other person is not going to be attracted to you automatically. You will have to appeal to the other person on the basis of some criteria other than your looks, and that can only happen if you get to know him or her better. You have to figure out some way to get that person to spend a little time with you, and the first step is to get to meet that person. For most of us this is not easy, and you may not feel comfortable doing it, but you have to do it anyway.

If you don't have the courage to do this directly, you need to get clever. Remember in the old romance stories where the lady would drop her handkerchief, right where the man would have to pick it up for her, so they could meet each other? That's exactly the kind of thing you want to do.

You need to practice up on your flirting techniques. Flirting has gotten a bad name over the years because it has been misused so much by people who were just teasing. That is unfortunate, because flirting really does serve a useful purpose. Flirting is basically just a way of telling someone that you find them attractive and that you are interested. Flirting conveys your attraction through eye contact, a nice smile, a touch on the arm. If you think that someone has pretty eyes, say so. Most people will feel complimented by your attention, and may respond with a return compliment. The purpose of flirting is to get past the first awkward steps in meeting each other.

If there is a special person whom you would like to meet whom you see on a regular basis, but you can't get up the courage to approach the person directly, figure out some excuse to have to interact with that person. Get on the same committee as that person. Schedule your lunch to be at the same hour as his or hers. Do your laundry at the same time if you live in the same building. Do one of these things this week and do another one next week. Do one again the following week. It may not get you anywhere, but you will never know unless you try. You have to give the other person the opportunity to decide about you, and you have to assist in the process.

Position yourself so that you are noticed. Here are some other things that you can do. Fabricate some circumstance that forces a conversation between you. Accidentally happen to be in the right place at the right time. Create a need or problem that the other person can help you with. Ask if he or she has change for the coffee machine. Ask for directions to some office in the building. If nothing else, ask if he or she has the time. Modify the circumstances so that it doesn't take too much courage in order to meet that special person. Do anything you can, but get something started!

Lots of bars provide an environment which is supposed to help you meet other people, and some do it quite successfully. But do the bar owners care one hoot whether or not you find a mate? Of course not. Self- interest is their real concern, the booze, food and services that they can sell to you at a profit. So, in the pursuit of making themselves a profit, they provide you with an environment which you are willing to pay for in the hopes of your meeting somebody interesting. Some bars have figured out how to do this very well, and generate a "standing room only" business for themselves.

I think one of the objections to the bar scene revolves around having an uncomfortable feeling that you're being evaluated on the wrong criteria. This environment strongly favors the men who are bold and the women who are either quite attractive or provocatively dressed. Those of us who are pretty average know we're going to have difficulty attracting the right person under these conditions.

Another attempt to provide services to singles in the past involved special travel events, such as singles cruises and ski trips for singles only. These days you can search on the internet. Search for "Meetup" and you will find groups that cater to all kinds of activities and interests. If your particular interest is not represented already, you can even start your own interest group.

Churches should be a good place for some people to look for a mate, and many churches do have single groups. The problem is in the numbers; the groups just aren't large enough to provide a good enough selection. The one church that has got this figured out is the Mormon church. In the greater Los Angeles area, they have set aside special wards just for singles, some catering to the younger singles, some catering to the older singles. Here again is an example of self interest. The Mormons want to help you find another Mormon to marry, so they set up this structure to help you out. The other churches either aren't as much motivated or haven't figured how to do this in an optimum fashion.

There are businesses that have also figured out how to appeal to singles in some of the most unlikely scenarios. In the Los Angeles area, people who get traffic tickets can choose to go to traffic school instead of having the citation recorded on their driving record. The traffic schools are not provided by the state, and are in fact private businesses. Since they have to compete for your business, some of them get pretty clever in devising ways to distinguish themselves from their competitors. Among the different categories of people they might try to attract, "singles only" is an obvious choice for some of them.

One of the best ideas I've seen for meeting people is called Table for Six, which apparently has been operating in Australia and New Zealand for several years and is now advertising in Los Angeles. Following a membership fee of $150, they will interview each member to determine interests, lifestyle and personal preferences. The organizers then match people in groups of six (3 men and 3 women) and arrange a dinner for them at some nice restaurant. Six turns out to be the optimum number of people: any more and it would be difficult to get to know everybody, and any fewer could make it uncomfortable and difficult to provide sufficient conversation to carry the evening. A service fee of $15 (in the LA area) is charged for arranging the dinner, and each person pays his/her own tab.

This could be a good program, since singles are always looking for someone to have dinner with. The $15 fee is within reason, the format is non-threatening, the security is not a problem, and it would be easy to either arrange or avoid a future get-together with someone you meet at the dinner. Whether this program will be able to attract enough people to provide a reasonable chance for you to meet the right kind of person remains to be seen.

Maybe you want to organize your own event. Lots of people have parties as a way of meeting people, but a friend gave me a new twist on this idea. Get ten of your friends who are single and arrange an after-work party that is scheduled to last only an hour or so. Each person has to bring someone of the opposite sex, a friend, a neighbor, a co-worker, who is not a date. If everyone does a diligent job of bringing good prospects to the party, you will meet ten first class candidates in the space of one hour. This format has several advantages, as you can see immediately. It's low cost, non-threatening, and balanced in male/female.

Historically, newspapers did their part by providing special sections with personal ads for those who wanted to advertise for a date, and there were even special publications printed solely for this purpose. Then, telephone services with 900 numbers were established so you could communicate by voice rather than by mail. In most cities there were single's clubs of one sort or another. These could range from free or low cost dances up to professional singles clubs. In Los Angeles, there were dating services you could join which provided video-taped interviews of the other members of the club, allowing you to do a significant amount of screening before you even arranged to meet somebody. The other party then got to review your file before agreeing to meet you. The Internet has now taken over this role as the most recent media to offer its services. With as large a single population as we now have, this process has gotten to be a fairly big part of the total dating scenario, and it is no longer considered the desperate last attempt to find love.

Even if a matching process itself were miraculously accurate, however, keep in mind the limitations inherent in this process. First of all, most of us are probably not very accurate about describing ourselves (many studies indicate that 95% of us will describe ourselves as above average).

Second, most of us have difficulty putting into words what we would really want in the way of a partner. Assuming that your potential candidate has the same difficulties, this means that there are four sources of error that any matching program would have a hard time dealing with. Third, these match programs can only match you against the candidates that are in their data files, and these files are of course always limited.

In the present internet environment, matching services have become commonplace and lots of people have used them. Some have become so popular that they are almost household words, such as Match.com, eHarmony, and OKCupid. They and all the other search sites perform the useful service of lining you up for dates with supposedly well matched candidates, and theoretically this should be a big help in your search for a perfect mate. However, PEW Research Center's Factank says that although one-in-ten Americans are now using one of the many online dating platforms, the vast majority of relationships still begin offline. Even among Americans who have been with their spouse or partner for five years or less, fully 88% say that they met their partner offline–without the help of a dating site.

Why are the results not better? Because compatibility as determined by a match-making company is only one part of your selection process; you also need compatibility on the personality and character issues discussed earlier in Chapter 5 on Compatibility. But in addition to compatibility, just as important are the dictates of Chemistry which determine whether or not you are attracted to each other. This adds another level of complexity which does not lend itself to rational analysis, so this aspect is not covered in this book. The solution to all these problems is to enhance your search routine and increase the number of candidates you consider as potential mates.

No matter what procedure you follow, you have to take advantage of the opportunities as you find them. A friend of mine is good looking enough that I thought she would have guys lined up to ask her out. But, she told me, she had trouble getting out to places where she could find men. Not only could she not cope with the bar scene, she couldn't even bring herself to join a ski club. So she spent a lot of Saturday nights alone. Fortunately, the story has a happy ending. She was working on a loan or insurance policy or something like that with an agent who was "kinda cute" and decided she wasn't going to let this opportunity get away. On the day they completed their work together, she summoned up all her courage and invited him for a glass of wine to celebrate. They are now happily married.

Sometimes there is no other way to do it but to just plain do it. I met my wife by walking over to her blanket at the beach, sitting down and starting to talk. It took all the courage I could muster to do that, but there was no other way. I don't know why it's so tough for all of us to do this, because all we are risking is a rejection, yet we all seem to have such a problem doing it. I can assure you that I would be much more able to do this now after years of being a salesman. It may not be easy, but if you can bring yourself to think like a salesman, maybe you will find the needed courage to do some of these things yourself.

If you have already searched for a while and still haven't succeeded, you might be discouraged about ever finding the right person. I don't know if it will make you feel any better, but your situation is similar to that of many salesmen. Think about how many doors the encyclopedia salesman has to knock on before he makes a sale. All of us in sales have to "work the numbers", and your situation is no different. You've got to make the number of candidates large if you want to find the right one. Even if you are not actively dating, never stop looking. Look at everyone you meet as a potential candidate, and don't give up on your search.

8

DATING

One of the things that you want to keep clearly in mind when you are searching for a mate is that there is a distinction between dating and marrying. Marrying is something you will hopefully do only once, whereas dating is something you will do dozens or even hundreds of times. That obviously means that you will date many whom you will not marry, and you want to approach dating with the right attitude.

I think it is helpful to realize that the dating process serves three separate purposes. The first purpose it serves is to help establish in your mind what other people are actually like. Only after you have dated for a while can you have some idea of what to expect from a member of the opposite sex in an intimate relationship. The more you date, the better equipped you are to determine what you want in a mate. Let's call this Mode 1, the learning period. I would arbitrarily put this period as being from age 16 to 25. In my own case, I think it took me until I was about 30 to get a handle on what I wanted out of a marriage and what I wanted in a partner.

The second reason to date is simply to have someone to share your leisure time with. Let's call this Mode 2. You may have started out thinking it wouldn't be much of a problem finding yourself a good mate, but you soon find out that that's not true. In fact, if you follow my advice and do a good job in selecting a mate, it could take a long time to find one. So you might as well enjoy yourself in the process. You will sometimes want to spend time with people who are acceptable enough for dating, even though you know full well that they probably won't qualify on your criteria for marriage. But what the heck - you gotta go out on Saturday night with somebody! Dating will at least get you out of the house, and you might meet someone else while you are out!

Thirdly, dating is how you determine whether or not any given person is a suitable mate for yourself. Once you have dated long enough to establish what criteria are important to you, dating is the way to get a close look at a candidate whom you would like to evaluate seriously. You could think of this as being a special kind of interviewing process, but of course it will involve some very intimate interviewing. And like any selection process, it may take a great many candidates before you find an acceptable one. Call this Mode 3, the evaluation period.

To summarize the three modes or phases of dating:

Mode 1: This mode starts with your first date and involves picking up clues as to what the opposite sex is like. You are only starting to think about what characteristics you might want in a mate, realizing that the search may be difficult.

Mode 2: In this mode you accept the fact that people you date do not have to be the marrying type. You are just dating because you need a companion. You keep one eye open for that exceptional candidate you hope will come along.

Mode 3: In this mode you have selected a candidate and are evaluating him/her according to the characteristics you have decided are important in a mate. This is the "going steady" mode, and if successful, leads to an engagement.

Much of the literature I've seen is written for female readers, and has to do with getting a man to "commit". Perhaps this might be explained more easily using the terminology I am offering here. Maybe the woman thinks she is in Mode 3, considering the man seriously, whereas the man doesn't feel she is the perfect mate and is only dating as a Mode 2 (casual) relationship.

When I think of courting behavior, the image that always comes to mind is the mating dance of some of the exotic bird species. The male struts around on his toes, fluffs up his feathers to look his prettiest, and sings some beautiful bird songs. He really puts on a show, and eventually, if he's lucky, the female is attracted to him. After he has been successful with the female, what does he do? He sits on the eggs and keeps them warm, a far from sexy assignment. I think there is a parallel in the dating scenario for humans.

Keep in mind that characteristics that you may enjoy or approve of in a date may differ from those you chose in a permanent mate. Singles like sports cars and convertibles. Marrieds drive sedans and station wagons. Being a good dancer can be a real plus as a single, but after getting married, it may be more important how good you are at changing diapers. The flashy ones may get more action during the dating process, but studies have shown that average people are more successful at finding a mate.

Given that the three modes of dating have three different objectives, you need to understand that there will be lots of occasions in which you will choose to date somebody whom you know is not perfect for you. There is no need to get anxious about this; just understand what you're doing.

If you are in the early part of your dating life, you should plan to be in Mode 1 for a while, during which you will be just trying to educate yourself about the opposite sex. Teenagers often don't understand this, and they suffer through the anguish of having relationships terminate which they just knew were going to last forever. Although the process is painful, this has to happen. Otherwise you wouldn't move on to the next love of your life and learn what you need to know about selecting a mate. As you get older, hindsight will make it easier to accept the fact that these relationships were not destined to become permanent.

After you get old enough and experienced enough to be looking for a permanent relationship, you will hopefully find a good candidate and move into Mode 3. In this mode you want to carefully evaluate this candidate against the criteria you have selected, and if you are satisfied, the search is over. If you are not completely happy with this choice, continue the search and try again.

Interviewing

I remember an incident relating to the subject of selection that happened to me years ago. A math-oriented friend of mine gave a group of us engineers a math puzzle that he hoped would stump us. His question was as follows: "Suppose you are interviewing and trying to hire a secretary from a group of 100 candidates, and you are given the restriction that you have to make your selection at the time of interview. How would you determine the best procedure to follow"? I wanted to make sure I understood the question correctly, so I asked "Oh, you mean you interview, say, 37 of them and then pick the best one that comes along after that?"

My math friend was so mad! He had hoped that we would have a hard time trying to figure this out, and there I had instantly blurted out what happened to be the correct answer. Must have been mental telepathy, I suppose, but somehow I had gotten the correct answer without even having had time to fully digest the question. He went on to tell us that if you have 100 candidates, 37 does in fact work out to be the optimum number to use in establishing the baseline, leaving you 63 more candidates from which to make your selection. (But he was so disgusted with me that he never did tell us how you could prove that this was the correct answer.)

Anyway, the numbers in this little story are not important, but the procedure is. This example is another way of explaining what I mean by Mode 1 dating versus Mode 2 dating. Mode 1 is needed to establish the baseline, a comparison against which any further evaluations will be made, the same way the first 37 secretarial applicants establish the baseline for the rest of the candidates. After the baseline is established, then you know what to look for during the rest of your interviewing, which is essentially what you will be doing in Mode 2 dating. Mode 2 fulfills your need for companionship while looking for Mr./Mrs. Right and a Mode 3 relationship.

Analyzing the dating process like this helps explain why young marriages so frequently end up in divorce. If you get married before you know what to look for, you probably won't make a very good choice. The average age at marriage has gradually moved up to the point where in 2016 the average age at marriage was 27 for women and for 29 for men. This implies that people no longer feel the pressure to get married too young, which is good. We all know of cases where young marriages have worked out just fine, but the chances are not as good as with later marriages.

If you have moved through Mode 1 so you know what to look for, found a good candidate and progressed into the courting phase in Mode 3 but it didn't work out, you're back in Mode 2. You are again dating with no immediate expectations of a permanent relationship. Mode 2 could last for years while you are searching for that ideal candidate, so prepare yourself for lots of casual dating relationships. Every now and then you'll find someone who warrants serious consideration, so you may slip back into Mode 3 again for awhile. But don't rush into a mistake. Learn to enjoy the process. Casual dating can be fun, too.

Women sometimes report that a guy they have fallen for turns out to be married, and they want some way to avoid this in the future. In response to this, some advisors suggest that you hire a private investigator, check his credit status, etc. I have an alternative suggestion, and mine is a lot cheaper. Remember my buying analogy. Smart buyers will ask for references, and you should do something similar. Meet his friends and see what they are like. If you are dating someone who never introduces you to any friends or people who know him well, that should raise a big flag.

Another clue would be that he doesn't ever invite you over to his place. If he says that you can't call him at his office, that's another clue. Nobody lives in a vacuum, and if all you have ever seen of his life is him, consider him married until he can prove otherwise.

Single Parent Dating

For single parents who are dedicated to raising their kids right and are involved in their activities, there isn't much time left for dating. Basically, if you commit to a schedule that takes care of the kids, you do not have a life! What can you do?

First of all, you have to accept that dating is not an activity designed for people with kids, and people with kids aren't supposed to be dating. No wonder you're having a tough time. Dating is a way to have fun while getting to know someone, but this time around you're more concerned about your kids having fun. Somehow, though, you still have to get to know your potential candidate. Using the same logic that says one plus one equals two, this means that your dating is going to have to involve your kids.

Parents Without Partners is an organization that understands this, and plans activities that involve you and the kids. But the same idea is appropriate even for dating on your own outside of *Parents Without Partners*. What's wrong with having a date that allows you to take care of your parenting duties at the same time?

Unless you are just looking for a fling, your list of requirements will now include that any potential mate must also like your kids as well as you, and be willing to spend time with all of you as a family. You don't have the luxury of dating any other type. But if you ever hope to remarry, your candidate will have to pass this test anyway, so this dating pattern is also a screening device. Anyone who won't date you in this fashion isn't likely to want to marry you either.

Actually, when you think about it, you'll get to know somebody a lot better after spending a day at the park, or at the little league field, or wherever, and then preparing dinner together. You get a full day with your kids, and your companion gets away with a cheap date. Leave time for "amore", and everybody wins.

Parting

In this process of searching for the mate of your dreams, you will get involved with a number of people who do not meet your criteria for the ideal mate. What this means is that, after some varying degree of involvement with these people, you will decide not to continue seeing them. Or maybe they will decide to stop seeing you. Let's call this parting.

The first thing to realize is that this has to occur. Unless you marry the very first person you ever date, you will have to go through parting. And the more people you date, the more parting you'll have to do.

I think parting is not fun. Love stories have been written for centuries about the agony endured by one or both parties when a breakup occurs in a relationship. Frequently one party is perceived as the bad guy and everybody grieves for the other. As uncomfortable as parting makes us all feel, though, it has to occur. This could happen after one date. It could happen after going steady. It could happen after being engaged. What we are trying to avoid is having this happen after marriage. Or worse yet, after kids.

Regardless of how your relationship progressed, it does not help to describe your dates, girlfriends/boyfriends, ex-lovers or ex-spouses in emotional and uncomplimentary terms. I suggest that instead you try to find a way to describe other people and your relationships with them in terms of the criteria described earlier. This may be hard to do initially, but if you can do it, it will be of considerable help in figuring out what it is you really want in a mate, and should help you in your search for the mate that you really want.

You see, in this way you don't have to necessarily make a value judgment about whether the other person is good or bad; you are only saying that his/her preferences and behavior are different from yours. What this does for you is to focus on what your own preferences really are. It allows you to look at these people as having been candidates for the position of "mate" who simply didn't qualify according to your criteria. If that last candidate wasn't suitable, you keep searching for one who is.

Isn't this a more pleasant way of looking at your dating situation? Now you don't have to say that the world is populated with a bunch of jerks, losers or weirdos. You simply say that it is awfully hard to find someone who meets your criteria. And you keep searching. But now you have an evaluation plan and an upbeat attitude. Doesn't this make you feel better?

Some people will suggest that you should be upfront and honest about why you are terminating a relationship. I would agree only under certain conditions: 1) If you have decided that you just aren't ready to get serious yet, 2) If you can point to some differences in criteria that aren't critical or judgmental. If it is because you had some negative opinion about that person, keep in mind that it is not your job to criticize or try to improve the other person. Your job is to find and select a mate for yourself, not to point out somebody else's shortcomings, which are only your opinion anyway. Try to ease your way out without hurting the other person's ego, similar to telling a salesman, "Thank you but I don't want to buy it" as nicely as you can.

It's not so bad if you do the parting, but if the other party terminates you, how do you react? Normally, most of us might feel deeply hurt, depending on how serious the relationship had been. We might have feelings of inadequacy, self doubts about our own worthiness, perhaps feelings of loneliness. I don't think there is any way around having those feelings. But I think if we put things in a new perspective, maybe those hurt feelings won't last as long as they used to.

Think back to the criteria that you are using to evaluate candidates for your selection of a mate. You have discarded any number of candidates as not meeting your criteria, haven't you? Well, sometimes the other person is going to do the same thing, but it's you who gets "dumped". It would be very normal to feel badly about your self worth, but it feels less badly if we put it in terms of mismatched criteria. Being dumped, so to speak, doesn't mean that you're an unworthy person. It simply means that one or more of your criteria didn't match very well with those of the other party. Wouldn't you rather find this out now, before things are too serious? If the relationship is not going to work, it's not going to work. Put this one behind you and get on to the next one. I predict that you will have lots of these situations before you find an acceptable mate, so there is no point in feeling too badly about it. Chalk it off to experience and move on.

Eventually you find that partings don't hurt so much any more. You realize that the search for the right person is indeed very difficult, and you'll just have to make the best of it while you continue to search. You no longer expect the next one to be the last one on your road to happiness. You can settle for less than you'd like on a date because you are a little more realistic about the chances of finding the perfect mate, knowing it may take a while. So now you can be a little more relaxed about dating, and just go out for the fun of it. Enjoy yourself, and keep trying.

There are lots of heartbreaks in life, actually, like losing a championship game, not being selected after interviewing for a job, or not getting the order after putting a lot of effort into trying to make a sale. The heartbreak in romance tends to make a better story and is the subject of countless books, but these are all disappointments we have to learn to deal with. Keep your chin up, and carry on.

A salesman learns with experience that although a sale seems to be progressing towards a close, something can always go wrong and ruin the sale. Your dating relationship is just like this. You have to continually monitor your progress to be aware of any signs that could mean that the sale won't go through.

Sadder but wiser is the familiar phrase that describes a person after a letdown of this kind, but I don't think we always get the message correctly. Just because you have a nice dating relationship doesn't mean it will end up in a marriage. Dating is easy to do and everyone does it, but marriage takes a serious commitment. A lot of people kick the tires and go for a test drive, but only a few end up buying the car.

Sex in Dating

I will draw your attention to some of the differences between men and women throughout this book, and sex is one of those differences. Women want to establish a relationship in order to decide if they want to have sex. Men want to have sex in order to decide if they want a relationship.

I was asked by a woman whether it is true that men expect sex by the third date. I told her that men typically don't discuss matters like this, so I didn't know what most men think. Since then I've seen the results of two surveys; in one the men gave a range of answers about how long they would wait for sex, in the other survey most men indicated they would be willing on the first date if the opportunity presented itself.

Margaret Kent has written an excellent book which you ladies must read, entitled *How To Marry The Man Of Your Choice*. With far more discussion than I'm giving it here, she says that a woman should have a dozen dates with a man so that they can get to know each other before they have sex. This way the woman can evaluate whether or not this is a man she wants to make an investment in, and if so, then she can include sex in their relationship. I think this may be good advice from a woman to a woman. But it is certainly one sided.

From a man's point of view, it's quite the opposite. A man wants to have the sex right away, and if it works out, then they can have a relationship. How many men would be willing to wait 12 dates before having sex is unknown, but it's clear that we have a significant difference of opinion here. Rather than trying to establish right or wrong, I would treat this like all the other criteria I've suggested and let compatibility determine the outcome.

Avoiding Pregnancy

Marriage should occur much later in life than it used to, so it is possible that you will engage in sexual activity before you get married. If you do, you must think about what you are doing, and plan ahead. There are lots of people who are opposed to this kind of advice, because they think that this kind of planning encourages sex. Whether it does or not I don't know. What I do know is this: they are not the ones who are going to get pregnant. You are. You let them do whatever they feel they ought to do. For yourself, just don't ever let yourself get into a situation for which you are not prepared.

The currently available birth control methods may not be perfect, but some have a very high probability of preventing pregnancy. But do you know why they fail? Because they don't get used! If it should happen that you do get yourself into this predicament, and you don't have protection, there is only one thing to do. Say no until you can be safe. There will be lots of other exciting moments in your life, so let this one pass you by. It only takes one mistake to ruin your life.

Not everyone will engage in sex, of course, and some will only have sex occasionally, but if you engage in sex long enough, your chances of having a pregnancy are high enough that you need to be concerned. Some birth control methods are considered very good, but that does not mean they are fool proof.

To help you understand how serious a problem this could be, let's make a rough estimate of the probability of pregnancy. Suppose that under the optimum conditions the probability of pregnancy with unprotected sex is one chance in six. Suppose that to protect yourself you use a birth control technique that is 90% effective, which means that it is 10% ineffective. Taking these probabilities together means that there is one chance in 60 that having sex will cause a pregnancy. If these numbers are realistic, having sex once a week carries the probability of one pregnancy within 60 weeks. That's just over a year!

Remember that these are probabilities we are discussing, not actual events, and probabilities can occur anytime. An event is just as likely to occur on the very first try as on the last try. The time to protect yourself is now, and every time hereafter.

Suppose that you are more careful about the female monthly cycle and your chances of pregnancy are only one in ten, and your birth control technique is 97% effective. Under these conditions your chances of pregnancy are theoretically only one in 300. Don't delude yourself into thinking that this means that you are safe. If you have an active sex life at the rate of once a week, this will only take six or seven years, and you stand a chance of three pregnancies between age 20 and 40! Be aware that seventy percent of the out-of-wedlock pregnancies occur to women 20 years and older.

All the studies about safe sex show that it is not a lack of knowledge, however, that explains the lack of use. It's a lack of discipline. Men should always use a condom because it serves as a birth control device as well as preventing the spread of sexually transmitted diseases. Women should have their own independent method of birth control in addition to what the men do, because using two birth control methods will obviously improve your chances of avoiding pregnancy. There are now lots of birth control methods to choose from, and it is important that you be well informed about them.

You should discuss this with your doctor, but you will have to be forceful and insistent if you want to get any useful information. You may wonder why the medical profession does not seem to take a very strong stand on this and actively promote birth control, but this is just another example of self interest. Doctors get paid to deliver babies and take care of sick kids, not for giving advice about cheap contraceptives. You will have to get your motivation from someone else, and here it is:

Men: If you think your pleasure may be reduced a little by using a condom, think how much more your pleasure will be reduced if you have to pay for an abortion or for 18 years of child support. In addition to the possibility of an accidental pregnancy, you can never be sure that she doesn't really, deep down, want to get pregnant, so protect yourself every time.

Ladies: You are the one who gets pregnant, so you're the one who has to make sure your sex is safe. You must plan ahead because you can never trust a man with an erection to be level headed. If you are not careful, you will spend the next 18 years of your life raising a kid. There is no guarantee that the father will stick around, so you may be doing this on your own. Don't get pregnant until you are ready!

9

THE DECISION

Making a decision to marry someone is obviously a very serious and difficult decision for anyone to make, and one that should not be taken lightly. There are books and books written on decision making, and hundreds, maybe thousands, of consultants who earn their living giving advice on how to make decisions, but somehow I don't think the standard advice is very useful in this case. I would like to propose a salesman's view of the decision making process, and see if it lends any useful insights into the decisions involved in selecting a mate.

I was a salesman, so I dealt every day with people who were evaluating and deciding. When I was trying to sell equipment, I usually had to answer a lot of questions about my product. Buyers who know what they're doing have a list of specifications that they want the equipment to satisfy, and they want to know how my equipment stacked up against their list. If my equipment couldn't satisfy their "specs", they didn't buy. You're doing the same thing when looking for a mate. You're the buyer with a list of criteria that you want satisfied.

In some respects, selecting a mate is like selecting a used car. Both come with a lot of history, and it is not easy to select a good one. Some will look flashy but have a poor interior. Some will look rather plain but will give you years of good service. Some will have defects that are easy to spot; others will have internal defects that won't surface for a while. A good one, however, if properly taken care of, will make your life much more enjoyable and comfortable.

The young buyers I run into typically don't know exactly what they want, because it takes experience to learn what's available and what criteria are important. Nobody can start right out and make smart buying decisions. The seasoned buyer, however, has a pretty good idea what he wants and has a much easier time selecting equipment that satisfies his needs. He has evaluated enough equipment to know what things are possible, and what things are important. If he has a specific function that the equipment must satisfy, and he can't find anything that satisfies that requirement, he doesn't buy anything at all. He saves his budget until a piece of equipment comes along that does satisfy his requirement.

Your procedure should be very similar. It may sound pretty cold-hearted to make a comparison like this, but I think the analogy is appropriate. Of course your feelings and other intangibles come into play along with the "facts", but I'm comfortable with the equipment analogy because equipment is not purchased on a strictly factual basis either. All sales courses for salesmen delve into the psychology of the buyer and other factors that are involved in a buyer's decision, and they point out that the buyer's personal makeup will be as important to the sale as the facts about the product being bought.

What I would like to emphasize, however, is that when it comes to making a decision about marriage, your experience in buying sweaters, cars or even equipment is not of much help. These decisions are too easy, and the cost of making a mistake is not high enough. But, how about buying a bank? How comfortable would you be if you were given the assignment to buy a bank? Where would you start? What criteria would you use? I would like to suggest that the decision on selecting a mate is at this level of difficulty, and should require about the same amount of study and planning. Decisions about a complex new situation don't come easily.

Obviously, nobody buys a bank without having made of lot of smaller decisions before that. A person has to build up to the big decisions of that magnitude. It's the same thing in your decision process looking for a mate. You start out with small buying decisions (asking for a date, or accepting a date). With a little more experience, you make bigger buying decisions (going steady). After lots and lots of experience of this nature, after learning what's important and what's available, then you may be ready to buy the bank. Of course, you have to wait for the right bank to come along; you don't want to buy just any bank! You follow this same process in your search for a mate.

Probably most people who are in the market to buy a bank know what a bank is and what the banking business is all about. You would expect that they will be well prepared to make their decisions, and know full well what the risks and benefits are. Can you say that about marriage?

What you hope is that, although your feelings may be emotional, your decision will be logical. The list of criteria in Chapter 5 should be the starting point in your selection process. Unless a candidate satisfies those criteria you've listed on your own personal criteria list, then that candidate is unacceptable.

However, I think it takes more that just those criteria to push you over the brink toward the decision. You have to feel good about the decision, too, and that may not be so easy to analyze with words. I think what I'm trying to say here can be best expressed by the words in a country and western song from 1989 by Tanya Tucker. It goes something like this:

> If it don't come easy
> you better let it go
> cause when it don't come easy
> there's no natural flow
> you might be better off alone.

The grammar could stand some improvement, but I agree with the message. Getting married is a big decision, and if you can't do it with complete confidence, don't do it. Perhaps we can sum it all up with the two questions that Dr. Joyce Brothers says you should ask yourself. Can I live with his/her faults for a lifetime? And would I rather be with him/her than anyone else in the world?

10

EXTERNAL EVENT

Knowing how difficult marriage can be, and how high the price is, it will take a lot of courage for a man to ask a woman to marry him. Even if he is sure he has found the right one. In my own case I was very conscious of the fact that I had found the right woman, but I still couldn't bring myself to pop the big question. Too much bravery required. I wanted to go on doing just what I was already doing, because that's easier than deciding to do something different. In life, as in physics, they call this inertia.

I remember well my personal experience with this back when I was dating my wife-to-be. I thought "This lady is as close to my ideal as I'll ever find, and I can't let her get away." I had already decided that this was the woman who met all of my criteria (although my criteria list was a little fuzzy back then), but I realized that it was going to be very difficult to bring myself to the decision point. Let's face it; asking someone to marry you is a very momentous decision. I remember very clearly what was going through my mind, and I realized I was in trouble.

If some external event didn't come along to push me over the edge, I'd probably never bring myself to ask her, and we would just carry on until something happened to break us up and I'd lose her. I was very conscious of what was happening, but that didn't make it any easier.

Fortunately, an event came along that was the excuse I needed. She was going to go back to North Dakota for her younger sister's wedding, and I knew she would feel uncomfortable being there as the older sister who was still single. Wouldn't it be a lot nicer if she could at least tell the home folks that she was engaged? Realizing that, I knew that if I were ever going to ask her, this would be the time. So I did.

Understanding that this is what happened in my case, I decided to check whether or not this is normal, or whether I represent some minority class of cowardly males. While I was writing this section I asked the first four business associates I came across about the circumstances involved in their own situations. Was there anything special about the timing of when they asked their wives to marry them? The first two said yes, they also had an external event that triggered the decision, and in both cases it was that they were going to move to another city.

The third said that in his case he had only been dating the young lady for about five weeks, but he was already sure that she was the one. She had apparently come to the same conclusion, because one night over an intimate dinner she had told him that she was going to marry him. After thinking it over for a week, he proposed to her. The fourth couldn't think of any special circumstances surrounding his proposal. So maybe my experience wasn't so unusual after all. In 4 of the 5 cases (including mine), some external event triggered the man's decision to go ahead and marry. My survey was far from scientific, but it continues to be supported in the many discussions I have had since then. Reflecting on the significance of this little study, I have concluded that an external event will be very helpful in getting someone to make a decision. If you are trying to get someone to make a decision, and there isn't an external event, create one.

Using the sales analogy again, salesmen take advantage of this phenomenon all the time using an external event to push someone into a making a decision, For example, there is nothing more effective than having a price increase coming up in the future to cause someone to buy now. Telling someone that you are about to run out of something is another way to get a decision in a hurry. A car salesman or a real estate person might tell you that someone else has already submitted a bid on the very one you have selected, and you'd better decide fast. And you probably will. Another example is having a discount that is available now that won't be offered later. There are lots of things that salesmen use to get you to make a decision, now.

If you are the salesman trying to make the sale, wouldn't you like to know the result sooner, rather than let the decision hang out there indefinitely? On the other hand, if you were going to lose the sale, wouldn't you also rather find that out sooner rather than later so you don't spend any more resources on a lost cause? In the equivalent marriage scenario, where a prospective mate has decided that he/she doesn't plan to ever marry you, wouldn't you rather know that as soon as possible so you can decide whether or not to continue the relationship? There are things you can do to force the decision.

Having either one of you move out of town is one of those external events that guarantees that a decision will get made; either it's a solo move or you decide to get married. Another external event would be a decision as to whether you'd like to invest your money in a house or condo, instead of paying rent. Investing together would make more sense if you were married, and it is an external event that could help force the decision. Even having the lease expire on your apartment will force you to decide whether to stay or move, and that can be used as your external event.

Ladies (and Men): Getting pregnant is frequently the external event that forces the decision, but that is not what I consider a good example of the right way to use this suggestion. While it may cause the marriage to occur, there will always be that cloud of uncertainty hanging over the marriage as to whether or not you really belong together. I can not emphasize this strongly enough. Do not allow pregnancy to occur and force the marriage decision. You'll pay for that mistake for the rest of your life!

Trial Close

There is a technique that every good salesman learns called the "trial close", which gives the salesman feedback on how he is doing in the process of trying to close the sale, i.e., get his sale completed. Using a trial close, a good salesman will test his customer every so often to see if the customer is still on track to make the decision to buy, but the trial close avoids having to directly ask "will you buy from me?"

For instance, if the salesman uses the trial close "How many will you be wanting to order?", and the customer responds with "We haven't decided for sure yet, but maybe a couple hundred", you know you're making progress toward the sale. If the customer responds "I'm not sure yet that this is what we will want", you know you have a lot more selling to do and the probability of a sale isn't very high.

You probably have used a trial close but didn't know that's what it was. If you are just meeting someone and you ask "Do you like to go to the movies?", that's really a trial close, intended to find out if he/she will go out with you. If the response is "yes, and there is a movie I really want to see sometime", you know you are on track. If the response is "I'm really too busy to go to the movies", you know there is an objection that you will have to uncover and eliminate or you are not going to make the sale.

If you have been dating for a while and you want to find out if there is any hope of having the relationship turn into a marriage, use a trial close. "If we were to get married, what would we do about .....". If the answer is something like "I don't plan on ever getting married", you know you don't have a chance. If the answer is something like "We can't get married until ......", then you know what the objection is and you can decide what to do to keep the sale progressing to a close. If the response is favorable, try another trial close, like "when do you think we should get married?"

If the answer is "How about June?", it's time to close the sale. "Oh, I'm so happy we're going to get married. Is it OK if I call my mother?"

Another example of a trial close could be "If we were to get married, would you want to live in a house or a condo?" If he/she says "I hate condos; they are too noisy. I think that we should get a house," that would be interpreted as a positive sign that you are on track. If he/she says" I'm never going to own either, because it restricts your freedom", you're probably not going to make the sale.

If you ask "How many kids do you want?", and the response is "How many do you want?", that would be a good indicator that you are progressing toward a sale. An answer like "I don't ever want any kids" answers the question about kids, but is inconclusive regarding the question of whether or not he/she will marry you. You need to redesign your trial question so there is less uncertainty about the meaning of the answer. If you ask "How soon do you think you'll want to get married?" an answer like "As soon as I finish grad school" would be a more positive indicator than "Not until I'm financially secure".

For you non-salesman readers to whom the trial close is a new idea, keep in mind that its purpose is to avoid the direct question, (are you going to buy? or in our case, are you going to marry me?) because if you ask the direct question too early, the answer may be negative. The purpose of the trial close is to see if there is even a possibility of a sale, and if there are any objections, to find out what they are. If you get a response that indicates that your customer is not ready to buy, you have more selling to do. After you uncover an objection and figure out how to eliminate it as an objection, then you look for any other objections by asking another trial close question. The trial close technique should be employed any number of times along the sequence of events until the decision is pretty much conclusive.

Not all sales efforts will end successfully, however, and you will not always make the sale. If you are set on getting married, and the "sale" is a marriage proposal, you still have to come to a final resolution, which is either yes or no. Keep asking trial questions until you find this out. If your trial close indicates that your candidate is not going to ever get married (to you) under any circumstances, you can stop wasting any more time on this candidate and move on to the next one.

It may also be worth mentioning that, in my very limited survey, in three out of five cases the woman mentioned marriage first. Once the subject of marriage has been broached, it then becomes an open topic for discussion and both of you should feel more comfortable about discussing it. I think this warrants further discussion. If the woman asks first, or tells him she is going to marry him, as with the third fellow in my story, think what this does. This relieves the man of a big burden of uncertainty. He no longer has to worry about being rejected if he asks her, because she has already indicated that she will say yes. For cowards like me, it may take one of those external events to get over that decision hurdle.

Conclusion: Use a trial close to find out if there is any hope for a positive outcome. If your candidate won't commit to a decision, create an external event that will force a yes or no answer.

11

COMPETENCE

Marriage can be thought of as an organization, albeit a small and very special one, and like all organizations, its success and survival will depend on the competence of its members. In my opinion, competence in marriage would include at least the following: understanding the differences between men and women and how that affects your relationship, having realistic expectations about what to expect in a modern marriage, selecting the right mate, and being skilled in communication, support, sex, and raising children.

The world has changed, and the reality of marriage has surely changed as well. It wasn't too many years ago that marriage was almost as inevitable as death and taxes, but that is clearly not the case anymore. More and more people are electing to remain single, and we need to analyze why that is. Who really should be married, and what qualifications should they have? Do you really want marriage, and how well could you cope with the strains on a modern marriage if you had one?

The book *How To Stop Looking For Someone Perfect and Find Someone To Love*, by Judith Sills, provides an excellent discussion about how many people use the wrong criteria for selecting a mate. When life was tough and physically challenging, criteria relating to biological survival were important. In our present environment of impersonal cities and uncertain futures, emotional survival may be much more critical. Marriage may help provide that support, but a good marriage will require competence.

Competence in Understanding Differences

Some of the differences between men and women are explained in the book *Opposite Sides of the Bed*, by Cris Evatt. One of the more critical, to my mind, is in regards to intimacy vs distance. She says that women need intimacy, although how much varies from woman to woman, and men need distance, which likewise varies from man to man. Where the problem really gets serious is when a woman with a high need for intimacy gets with a man with a high need for distance. Or when women have unrealistic expectations about intimacy and men have unrealistic expectations about distance. She quotes James Harper, a family therapist at Brigham Young University, as saying "What's important is being satisfied with the amount of intimacy you have. Every relationship sets its own level of intimacy. There's no optimal level".

If women understood how much men fear being engulfed and smothered, maybe they would understand why it is so hard to get a man to commit. A woman needs to figure out how to avoid feeling lonely, sad, desperate, and anxious when a man wants distance, and the man needs to learn how to give her the reassurance that she is not being abandoned. If a couple has this problem, she will want to talk about it, because that in itself is intimacy. And he'll want to avoid any serious discussion for the same reason. Competence means understanding this difference and finding a way to satisfy both parties.

I find it easier to understand why men and women do what they do, and why they are different, if I visualize a scenario with a caveman and his environment from the distant past. Remember that the human species has existed for several million years, slowly evolving into what is now our modern physiological configuration, but our densely populated urban living environment is only a few thousand years old. Technology, crowding and the urban environment have created problems that our human and social development has not been able to keep up with.

"Cavemen" had to be independent and resourceful in order to survive in a very dangerous world outside the "cave", whereas "Cavewomen" did the household chores around the cave and had to learn how to develop close relationships with the other women in the clan. It's easy to see how men and women would develop differently, and I think there is a limit to how much you can expect the opposite sex to accommodate your way of doing things. What we need is more tolerance and understanding. When these bothersome differences come up, remind yourself of the caveman scenario and try to realize how recent that was in the evolutionary time frame.

Some changes have occurred, but men and women are still quite different. It may be possible to get a man to do a woman's chores, or to get a woman to do a man's chores, but I don't think you can get one to think like the other. It just may be that a woman is more sensitive to a baby crying in the night, and will worry about how the kids did in play group today, whereas the man is more likely to worry about teaching junior how to avoid becoming somebody's lunch the next time they go out on a hunt.

This caveman scenario has been reasonably appropriate until very recently. Women working outside the home as equals to men has only existed during the last 50 years or so; is it any wonder that we haven't learned how to do it perfectly yet?

Competence in Expectations

Our image of the model American family for the last 50 years or so has been the nuclear family, with mom and dad and a couple of nice kids living in suburbia. Dad went off to work in the morning and mom stayed home to take care of the kids and the household.

Our environment has changed dramatically, however. Our cities are now much bigger and more densely packed, jobs are not so permanent and people have to move a lot, and it takes more than one income to support a middle class life style. Women are increasingly more independent and can earn good incomes, and men are asked to be more sensitive and caring. It isn't the same old world anymore. Our expectations need to fit the current realities. Here's a column from Ann Landers to start you thinking.

> DEAR ANN: That letter signed "Growing Uneasy in L.A." could have been mine. She asked whether she should marry "Greg," a great companion and lover but not eager to look for work. The only difference between her and me is that it's too late for me. I'm already married to "Greg." I've spent a lot of time and energy trying to motivate, encourage and psych out my husband, but nothing works. He's had a few jobs, but they didn't last long. I was raised to stick with my commitments so divorce is out. But when I think of

myself growing old and gray and broke, I wonder if having an errand boy, a few laughs and good sex is worth it.

Tell "Growing Uneasy" to find someone else before she gets stuck with an albatross. __ CARETAKER IN VA

DEAR VA: I did, and I really got clobbered by the male Establishment of North America. They labeled me "a female chauvinist oink oink." Read on for a closer look at what I've been getting.

FROM LOS ANGELES: If women are to be liberated from housework, men should be freed from unrealistic expectations of financial block-busting. Not every woman is Suzy Homemaker, and not every man is Bill Gates. Be fair, for Lord's sake.

NEW ORLEANS: That woman who makes $65,000 a year, pays all expenses and gives Greg an allowance should not have been criticized. Greg, she said, is attractive, intelligent, a great lover, and totally faithful. He runs errands and helps with the marketing, cooking and cleaning. The question was asked, "Is he a lazy parasite?" Why isn't a woman who stays at home considered a "lazy parasite"? Where's your sense of fairness?

CHICAGO: What kind of sexist garbage are you handing out these days? Here is a decent, well-behaved man who treats his woman beautifully and helps around the house, and the only problem is he doesn't have a job. If the situation were reversed, and a man had written that letter, you would have told him to shut up and count his blessings. Before equal rights, women stayed at home and men supported them. I never heard a man complain. "Growing Uneasy" should reel that guy in before someone else grabs him.

This is an example of where realistic expectations fit in. Does she really expect a superman? If the man being described were this good, and also had the drive and ability to hold down a high paying job, do you think he would be attached to this lady? Fat chance! My bet is that he'd be married to Miss America.

On the other hand, his expectations are unrealistic as well. He thinks that being a wonderful house pet is all he needs to contribute in order to fulfill his end of the bargain. While it is doubtful that he could match her level of income, it appears that she would accept even a modest level of effort of his part.

Go back to the three criteria you said that you absolutely have to have in a mate and see if those are really the ones that will make you happy. Some of the characteristics that you want may come at the expense of some of the others, and you have to know what trade-offs you are willing to make.

Competence in Selecting a Mate

I must insert a caveat here. The logical discussion of marriage and mate selection makes sense only if you are a reasonably rational person who was able to grow up without too many psychological hangups. If you grew up in a dysfunctional family, you may need to get yourself straight before you can attract and hold the right kind of mate. If you can look in the mirror and say that you are perfectly okay, you can ignore this section.

In one of the many letters to Ann Landers that I have read, a woman talked about her bright, talented and attractive daughter who always went for the men who were emotional and verbal abusers, liars and cheats. It turned out that the problem was due to the fact that the husband of the writer, i.e. the girl's father, was exactly that type of man himself. The mother had finally gotten herself out of her awful marriage, but she was afraid that the daughter was destined to make the same mistake herself.

If you suffered through childhood with emotional problems, marriage will be very difficult. Solve these problems first, then come back and look at this discussion with the hope of finding a lasting, happy relationship. Make sure you get help before you become a parent so there is less chance that you might pass these problems on to your kids.

It is also critical that you avoid selecting a mate who shows evidence of serious psychological or emotional problems. If you are a divorcee who already has children, be especially careful. Men do not always form an attachment for children who are not their own flesh and blood, and are fifty times as likely to be abusive as natural fathers.

Let me use a sales analogy to help you formulate a position on this issue if you have a serious concern about a possible mate. If you are considering buying a car, and the car breaks down during a test drive, what would you think? Wouldn't you worry about how much worse will it be with a few more miles on it? Pass on this one and look for another.

Lots of people have little behaviors or idiosyncrasies that are distracting or annoying, some of which can be changed and some can be tolerated. However, you need to be aware of the more serious behaviors which are not easily cured and which you should not tolerate in a mate. Child abuse, drug abuse, violence, and alcoholism all have well documented histories of repeating themselves from one generation to the next. My list would also include compulsive gambling, and excessive jealousy and possessiveness. In my opinion, all of these indicate a personality that has not been fully developed, and there will be nothing predictable about your future except the heartache and the agony.

When the thrill of a new love wears off, the violence and other problems will still be there. Look for warning signs of these problems. That's what a test drive is for, to give you a preview of what to expect. Don't think you are going to fix these defects and character flaws. You can see what's coming, and you don't need it. Walk away from it.

Competence in Communication

Here is an introduction to the subject based on an article in the Los Angeles Times, referring to studies on communication done by Deborah Tannen for her book *You Just Don't Understand: Women and Men in Conversation*. Women expect their men to be like a girlfriend, to listen to everything that whizzes through their brains. They use talk to connect. Men, although they are prepared to talk for recreation, prefer to use it to negotiate or solve problems or raise their status. Women are incredulous that men do not exchange personal information with their friends, whereas men are incredulous that many women are willing to share intimate details so easily. An example from the article: "One day the author said to her husband, "I'm thirsty." At first he responded by offering to solve her problem. "I'll get you a glass of water," he said. But then he realized he had fallen into what her life work has shown to be a typically male trap: instead of giving her sympathy he tried to solve her problem. "Oooooh I'm sorry," he quickly added. "You know, I was thirsty once. I know what that feels like."

I hope this explanation will be as useful for you as it was for me. I have since read her entire book and recommend strongly that you do the same. Instead of assigning fault to the other person for your communication problems, you need to know that communication difficulties are partly due to the differences between men and women. Reading this book will help you understand and accept those differences.

Competence in Supportiveness

If marriage is to provide the emotional support we all want and need, each spouse will have to be competent in understanding what the other needs. I don't think it is at all easy to understand what this involves. Boys and girls in our society spend the first two decades of life trying to learn how to grow up to be successful as men and women. During that time we are taught to tolerate the opposite sex, but our interactions with them are either superficial or gender neutral. Once we get into the marriage relationship, however, we are somehow supposed to know how to deal with the opposite sex on a daily basis at the highest level of intimacy. We never really get trained in how to do this, so we don't understand why our interactions don't always turn out the way we would like.

The problem is that men and women communicate differently and interpret things differently. We don't understand the other sex. What we need is an interpreter or translator. I think you will find the book *Men Are From Mars, Women Are From Venus* by John Gray, PhD, very helpful in this regard. Learning to be more sensitive to the gender differences he describes will help you be more caring and supportive of your spouse, and should greatly improve your relationship.

Competence in Sex

Ellen Kreidman says in an article in *Family Circle* that couples often complain that they are unhappy with the frequency of their love making. Usually, the woman complains that it's too often and the man complains that it's not enough. She says that men and women are different, and that each must understand the other's basic needs and do everything possible to fulfill them.

Men, she says, do not have a clue how emotionally starved most women are. And if the man is not competent at meeting her emotional needs, it is almost impossible for her to respond sexually. She wants kindness, gentleness, devotion, commitment, attention, patience and compliments. Her desire for sex results from feeling cared for, cherished, and loved. A woman whose mate takes the time to let her know that she's special, needed, appreciated and loved will be far more available sexually than a woman who is neglected or ignored. Kreidman says that women who hate sex are the same women who wind up having affairs with men who give them the affection, attention and conversation they've been craving for years.

She says that women, on the other hand, truly don't understand how strong a man's sex drive really is. Every man wants to feel wanted and needed physically. A man whose mate simply tolerates sex feels diminished both sexually and emotionally and is likely to seek a sexually satisfying relationship elsewhere.

Other authors have pointed out another difference: Men want sex in order to relax, whereas women have to be relaxed in order to want sex. If a marriage is to be successful, these differences have to be understood, and the partners may have to extend themselves at times to satisfy each other.

Competence in Raising Kids

After you do get married and decide to have kids, consider some of the decisions that married partners have to make. It would seem that, in some respects, picking a partner in marriage is not all that different from picking a partner in business. Basically the success of either type of partnership boils down to whether or not the partners have the same goals, the same objectives, the same vision.

The business partnership has to earn an income, keep from going broke, and produce a product that other people will want. The partnership in marriage can be thought of in exactly the same way with one major difference; in the marriage partnership, the product is kids. It is interesting to consider the fact that the production of children is probably the least regulated of all manufacturing enterprises in the US. There is no control over the quantity of children produced, nor over the quality of the children produced. In the case of unmarried parents, the production is not even licensed!

In the business partnership, if the product is not satisfactory and nobody wants the product, the partnership dissolves and you throw the parts away. You certainly don't want to get into this kind of a marriage partnership, or worse yet, an unmarried partnership, in which the kids get treated in this way. Make sure your marriage partnership has the greatest chance of survival by marrying the right person the first time.

Much of what kids learn they don't learn in school. They learn it from their moms and dads, and it takes both of you to do it right. Although women may be superbly capable of taking care of babies, eventually those babies grow up. There are a number of things that a man contributes to the rearing of children once they become ten years and older, especially the boys. In addition to serving as a disciplinarian, a role model, and a coach, the man approaches the parenting role from a different perspective.

Women tend to give love unconditionally, whereas men tend to put some performance requirements on their love. If the kids have a dad, they have to learn how to become good citizens if they want to meet with their dad's approval. There is far less control over how they grow up if a single mom has to do it all by herself.

Secondly, the boys need to have a successful man around whom they can emulate. How can a boy learn how to be a man if all his role models are women? And for the girls, it is probably better if they get a balanced view of the world by seeing how a man reacts and handles things, not just how another woman (mom) does it.

Third, boys need to develop skills in order to become successful men, and good fathers are full time coaches about every aspect of growing up. Mom tells the kid to be careful, whereas dad encourages the child to challenge himself (or herself). Fathers can offer a man's perspective on life's events which may be quite different from mom's view of things. When you get right down to the truth of the matter, a child needs both parents.

Raising kids without abuse takes a tremendous amount of parenting skills, and people who grew up with parents who were abusive did not have good role models to follow, and probably never learned how to interact successfully without resorting to violence. People like this shouldn't have kids, and you certainly don't want to marry one if you can help it.

There are other behaviors that you will also want to be concerned about. In some cases the man runs off because he can't stand to make the effort required to raise the family and/or keep it together. On the other hand, a woman can cause an even worse problem if she bears a child while being a user of tobacco, alcohol or drugs during pregnancy. Kids can be born with a drug or alcohol dependency which usually destroys any chance of their developing into normal healthy children.

The world as we find it today is a difficult place to live in, and your kids will need all the help you can give them. If you're not concerned with how well your kids will turn out, you should be. Remember this: your kids are going to have to compete with my kids.

12

SO WHO WANTS TO MARRY YOU?

In previous chapters we discussed how difficult it is to find the right mate. If you impose 20 criteria with a 50% probability for each, the odds are one in a million of finding someone who satisfies all of them. To make matters worse, in the foregoing analysis, you were doing the selecting according to the criteria you had selected. To be realistic, we would also have to consider that the 50% factor works both ways, and only half of those candidates might want you!

It's a sobering thought to realize that, before you can get married, you will have to pass somebody else's acceptance test. Doesn't that set you back? After you've gone through all this long, drawn-out evaluation process of figuring out who the right mate is for you, you have to realize that the others are using that same process on you! How well will you do?

If you look around, you will see married people who are tall, short, fat, skinny, dumb, smart, rich, poor, all kinds of people who are married. In other words, there's a chance for anyone to get married. But remember, the goal isn't just to get married, but to get married right. Let's face it. Most of us are more or less average. That's ok. Millions of us have learned to live with that. But remember, this applies directly to your search for a mate. You do have to be somewhat honest with yourself so you don't delude yourself into a futile search for something you'll never find.

Selling yourself is not much different from selling anything else. You are the product to be sold, and the "price" you are asking is the quality of the partner you are trying to attract. Put yourself in the position of a salesman who is trying to talk someone into buying a product, and the product is you. What could the salesman say good about you? What problems would he run into trying to explain away some of your lesser qualities? Are any of these characteristics things that can be and should be improved upon?

One female writer to Ann Landers was lamenting the fact that the chances of meeting a man over 30 who isn't married, an alcoholic, a moocher or gay are pretty slim. A male respondent countered that the females he has met almost all have serious psychological problems, and he has been shocked by the number of women who have very little to offer yet consider themselves some sort of prize. To some extent, they may both be right. Maybe a lot of people do have unrealistic evaluations of themselves.

You probably think you're something special, and it is critical that you think that. It is also very helpful if your parents think that. But why should anyone else think you are special? What do you have to offer so you can attract the "best" possible mate? If you weigh 230 pounds instead of 180, you will probably attract a mate who weighs 170 instead of 130. If you are a college dropout, you will probably attract the same. If you've got spiked green hair, your choices are probably limited to those few others who also prefer to exhibit some outlandish personal appearance. In other words, to some degree, you get what you deserve.

Or maybe you deserve what you get. I'm not trying to insult you here. I'm just trying to get you to be realistic. If you're already perfect, you can ignore all of this.

Regardless of what you have to offer, you can be comforted by the thought that there is someone for everyone. Consider this letter to "Dear Abby".

> Dear Abby: Regarding the letter from "A Loser in Kansas", may I contribute a little input from my own experience? I am also an average-looking 35-year-old man who has never been married-although I, too, want to meet the right woman. I am also paralyzed from the waist down, partially incontinent and basically impotent. (Just what every woman is looking for, right?)
>
> But in the 10 years since my becoming "disabled," I have had three wonderful relationships, emotionally and sexually. My motto: "If what you got don't work, work with what you got." Like you said, Abby, "If you label yourself a loser, you will never be a winner."

With an attitude like that, you know he'll eventually find his true love. A person like that makes it hard for you to feel sorry for yourself, even if you do have some features that keep you from being perfect. If you were going to sell a used car, you would probably do those little things that help it sell better, wouldn't you? You'd put on some new tires, give it a new paint job, and make sure it was washed and waxed. There are some equivalent things you should do while trying to sell yourself.

By comparing you to a used car, I don't mean to imply cheap. A used Rolls Royce is by no means cheap. What I mean by the used car analogy is that you already have a lot of miles on you. An outsider doesn't know what your history is and what your experiences have done to you or for you. You need to present yourself as best you can. Develop yourself to the level at which you can be proud of yourself. A salesman can only be successful if he believes in his product, so make your product the best it can be. See if any part of the following suggestions would be helpful.

Finish your training!

There are a great many people who start college or some special training program but don't finish. Some get close to completion, then get bored or disgusted with school and figure that they've gotten the benefit of all the useful coursework so they can quit early without finishing. This is a situation I am very familiar with, because I used to interview people who were in this situation. I want you to know that there is a tremendous penalty attached to non-completion.

The world has gotten so complex and impersonal that it is impossible to know everything first hand, so there are established standards to help us evaluate things that we can not test for ourselves personally. In education, that's why there are certificates of completion for shorter programs, and degrees for longer programs. If you terminate a program without the certificate or degree, nobody knows for sure what to think. Generally, we are not very accepting of people who don't finish things, and that includes educational programs.

In case you don't think you operate this way, consider these examples. Would you choose to be operated on by a doctor who didn't quite finish medical school? Would you choose to fly with a pilot who never quite finished flight school?

You might be enjoying an income that satisfies you for the moment, but it may leave your future at risk. Keep in mind that you are going to have to work for another 20 or 30 or 40 more years. You may not be concerned about how employable you will be in the future, but your kids will sure be. Everything that I read says that the job openings of the future will be for "knowledge workers", and these jobs will require higher levels of skill and training. Your employability in the future will depend on how you keep up with your training and education, and your eligibility for that further training and education depends on what you have achieved thus far.

Don't ignore the fact that your earning capability will be one of the factors on which you are judged by any potential mates. Make the effort while you are young and single. Evaluate your current standing on the educational ladder, and move it up a notch or two. You'll get a better mate as a result.

Improve yourself

Employment in our complex, high tech world is not getting any easier to obtain, nor to hold on to. It would be wise to put some extra effort into your career while you're still young and energetic enough to work those extra hours. Do whatever it takes to improve your skill level so you will be employable in the future. Graduate school is no longer an option reserved just for the very rich or very smart, and you would do well to consider an advanced degree while you have only yourself to support.

Besides age and position, there are other status factors that could be improved upon while being single. One obvious status factor is money. I think that most of us would agree that, all other things being equal, a potential mate with some money is more attractive than one with less money. So perhaps while you're single you can work toward putting a little money in the bank. Besides, once you get married and have kids, it's doubtful that you'll have much of an opportunity to save money for a while, and you'll be glad you saved up beforehand. As Christopher Marlowe has said, money can't buy love, but it can improve your bargaining position.

Achieve Status Congruence

Status congruence means that all your status factors are consistent with each other, i.e. they are all at the same level. Other people will be more comfortable dealing with you if you have status congruence, so you want to analyze your status factors to see if yours are congruent.

Let me explain with an example of status "incongruence". Imagine that you are scheduled to meet the president of a major Fortune 500 company. What is your image of what this person will look like? Maybe you imagine a tall, attractive man, very self confident, well spoken, impeccably dressed, knowledgeable about his field, etc. Suppose that when you meet him you discover that he does in fact fit all of your expectations except for one. He is twenty two years old!

This is an example of status incongruence. One of his status factors does not fit (is not congruent) with all his other status factors. Having this status incongruence causes a problem. How do you treat this guy? Do you treat him as a president, or as a 22 year old kid? This particular problem does occur in real-life situations which you have perhaps seen. In some cases there is a truly amazing youngster who earns a position well above his/her years. But there are other cases where a kid has a high ranking position because the kid's father is the boss, and everybody knows that the kid would never deserve this position on his own merits. In either case, you are never quite sure how to relate to the person, because his age and his other status factors aren't congruent.

Status incongruence for some reason makes us all feel uneasy. Another example would be an athlete who has won several world championships but has never won the gold medal at the Olympics. We feel sorry for our pro athletes who have won everything but a championship. For some reason we just feel better when everything lines up, and we wish he/she could win just one more time in order to make his/her career complete.

Another way to explain this would be to think of a report card which has all A's and one C, which is somehow unsettling. It makes you wonder why the student couldn't get that C up to match the rest of his/her grades.

Hollywood has apparently observed this phenomena and has come to this same conclusion. The result is that lots of people have resolved this issue by getting face lifts, tummy tucks, nose jobs, breast enhancements, toupees, having their teeth capped, etc., even having their names changed, in order to eliminate any single characteristic that did not fit in with an otherwise perfect appearance.

Most of us can ignore this advice because we don't have this problem. Most of us have an equivalent personal report card that has some A's and some B's and some C's, which makes us more of less normal, and other people accept us as having some characteristics that are better than others. This particular advice regarding congruence is intended only for those few who have all A's except for that one C which they should fix.

If you have a single status factor that is lower than all your other status factors, do what you can to raise it up to the level of the others. Get rid of that one thing that brings you down. That way people can deal with you at the average level of all your status factors, without having the discomfort of having to deal with that one low status factor.

The example of status incongruence that I especially want to address has to do with education. I used to deal with administration and personnel affairs for a large aerospace company. In this company, (and in most companies like it I'm sure), there were always some employees who were superb in every way but did not have a college degree. While everybody agreed that these people had the skill, experience, and dedication to do a fine job, the company rules stated that the positions they held required a degree. For their entire careers, these people will have to fight the problems associated with being "exceptions" to the employment guidelines set forth by their personnel departments. Everyone would be much more comfortable if these people would just get a degree so that all their status factors were congruent. This advice applies whether your situation requires an AA degree, a BS or a PhD. Finish that degree!

It is also possible for a person to have one status factor that is out of line in the positive direction, i.e. one high status factor but no others. This is the report card with all D's and one A. Examples could include some rock stars and professional athletes or the proverbial spoiled rich kid. We just don't know exactly how to treat these people because they have status factors at two levels. Keep this in mind if you find yourself infatuated with someone who has achieved the kind of success that comes as a result of a single factor that is exceptionally high. Remember that you have to live day to day with all the other factors as well. These other factors could be quite average, or even below average, and some could be quite incompatible with your other preferences in life. Teenage groupies at a rock concert fit the example of falling for someone on the basis of a single high attribute, but with luck they will probably grow out of it.

Exceptionally beautiful women have two problems in this regard. The first is that they tend to be suspicious that men love them only for their beauty, and they will frequently be right. The second is that they may have become accustomed to getting everything they want with very little effort, and have not had to develop the other aspects of personality that are necessary in a fully rounded person.

If you happen to be the one who has a single high status factor, you obviously wouldn't want to discard the exceptional factor, even though it is out of line with your other status factors. But status incongruence, even if it is due to a high status factor, causes discomfort. So if you have it, fix it. Popular athletes and entertainers, for example, achieve balance by elevating their other status factors. If you are lucky enough to have a high status factor, try to elevate some of your other status factors.

Look Your Best

Keep yourself as attractive as possible, because you never know when you might meet that special candidate. Being overweight is a common problem for both men and women, and it takes discipline to overcome. While you may be able to justify it to yourself, you can't make somebody else like it. Keep in mind that every little bit of improvement increases the range of candidates who might be willing to consider you as a mate.

Some people think they can improve their looks by being fashionable. That may be enough for some people, but it won't satisfy everybody. How fashionable can you be after you take your clothes off? That's the test you will eventually have to pass, so maintain yourself accordingly.

Improve your personality

In our society, we do lots of things to improve ourselves, and I'll bet you do, too. You go to the gym to improve your body. You go to the doctor to improve your health. You go to school to improve your mind. What have you done to improve your personality? Probably nothing.

This advice is especially important to anyone who has trouble relating to other people, but I think many of us have some personality traits that are less than ideal. I think almost all of us could use a good dose of behavior modification that would make us more like-able, more pleasant, more courteous, more helpful, more lovable.

I doubt that you would agree to get a complete personality makeover, even if such a thing were possible, but maybe you will agree to this one realistic suggestion for personal improvement which could make a big difference in your life. In fact, it may be my most important piece of advice to you. I suggest that you sign up for a Dale Carnegie course, or something similar, on how to win friends and influence people. I think you will be amazed at how much more interesting and likable you will become, and how much more successful you will be in dealing with people.

If you have a pretty average personality, this course will greatly increase your chances of being liked and accepted, and will greatly improve your dating life. If you have a fairly nice personality already, this course will make you even better.

Engineers and Scientists: Even if people think you are intelligent and nice and have good earning potential, the stereotype is that you are rather dull and uninteresting, whether it is true or not. Improve your interpersonal skills with a Dale Carnegie course. This should make you much more attractive as a mate, as well as doing wonders for your career.

All men: My casual survey indicates that an incredibly high percentage of women say that they want a man who has a sense of humor. If I could figure out how to teach this, I could get rich instantly. Since I can't, my best free suggestion is that, after taking the Dale Carnegie course to improve your personality, you join Toastmasters to improve your speaking skills and develop your confidence.

13

BENEFITS OF DELAYING MARRIAGE

If you follow my advice and do a thorough job of searching for the proper mate, the search could take a while. Mine took twelve years, counting from when I was graduated from college at 22 until I met my wife-to-be when I was 34. Regardless of how long it takes you, I think you will benefit from delaying marriage until you are really ready.

First, the obvious benefits: 1) you're older and wiser and more patient so you will do a better job of parenting 2) you have more money so you can afford a better lifestyle for yourself and your kids. Now, with the advantage of hindsight, I feel there are other benefits that are more subtle.

Particularly for men, age is one of your personal status factors, and you are gaining status even as you wait and grow older. The benefit of having higher status is that you can attract a higher status mate. Men especially need to be concerned with having a well paying job, because 77% of the women think it is an important and essential requirement for a spouse. For the most part, you will probably qualify for a better mate simply by taking the time to make a thorough search while looking for the right mate.

Some of the things you might want to do in life require a tremendous amount of time and/or effort, and many of these would be easier or better to do on single status rather than after getting married. An example would be getting your military service out of the way, or doing a stint in the Peace Corps, or the Job Corps, or getting involved in any extended training program which would be more convenient to do while single. I think attending college is in this category. Graduate school might even be affordable while you have only yourself to support.

Employment is so uncertain anymore that it would be wise to get yourself at least somewhat established before encumbering yourself with the additional obligations of a family. And if wealth is important to you, get your start while you are young and single and still in charge of your own finances. If travel is of any interest to you, this is a good time to do it. Travel is a lot cheaper when you're young and single.

Now on top of all that strictly logical stuff, I think you should delay marriage and enjoy being single because being single is fun. There will never be another time in your life when you have such a good opportunity to do fun things. With nobody to tell you what to do! Why transition from having your parents tell you what to do, to having your teachers tell you what to do, to having your spouse tell you what to do? Why not enjoy this period when you, and only you, are the boss. This should be an enjoyable time in your life and there is no reason to arbitrarily try to shorten it. You have fifty more years as an adult during which to get married and raise a family. That's certainly the way I felt. It was a conscious decision on my part not to ever get married until being married was better than being single. And I was 35 before that happened.

However, just because you are going to be single for awhile doesn't mean you necessarily want to be alone. A new set of studies about happiness has discovered something highly relevant to our discussion about marriage. These studies have found that the number one contribution to happiness is having close relationships. The second highest contributor to happiness is a happy marriage. Supportive, intimate connections seem to be very important as a source of happiness.

What this says is that one of the most important things you can do is to have a good friend, especially if you are single. This seems obvious, but apparently many people don't have a really close friend, not even one. Those who have two or three are really lucky.

A friend is someone who likes you in spite of yourself. A friend withholds judgment, and accepts you the way you are. A friend is always supportive, no matter what. For my own personal definition, a friend is that special person I would call if I were in jail in Mexico and they allowed me only one phone call.

Finding a good friend is only a little bit easier than finding a spouse. From my observation, friends are those with whom we have shared some significant experience. For some, it's your high school buddies. For some, it's your army buddies. For others, it's your fraternity or sorority buddies. For some, it's those few people at work with whom you have shared many years of headaches, deadlines, and successes. The problem is that in our current highly mobile society, you get separated from your friend(s) and you find yourself alone again.

Concentrate on developing one close friendship, if you don't already have one. Life can be much more bearable if you have a friend. If you can work it so you have more than one, even better. When you have a really good friend, the search for a mate doesn't have the same sense of urgency, because you can get some emotional support from your friend. That will allow you to take your time trying to find a mate, and do it right, which could take a while.

For lots of people these days, marriage may never happen, and I think that's okay too. For some, looking for the right mate may be like the search for the holy grail; it never ends. Keep in mind that being married isn't necessarily the only way to be happy. Being married simply means that sex, companionship, and partnership all come from the same person, your mate. Even if you stay single, though, you can still have sex and companionship, and you don't need the partnership. Keep in mind that being single, even if it makes you a little unhappy, is certainly better than being married to the wrong person and being a lot unhappy. Or worse yet, think how awful it would be trying to cope with alimony or child care payments. Don't let that happen to you. Enjoy being single, and keep on searching.

Clearly women can afford to wait longer now than before, because the men are waiting. Since the average age at marriage has been gradually increasing and is now about 27 for women and 29 for men, this obviously means that some are considerably older than this when they marry.

Ladies: Just because you are ready to marry doesn't mean the men are. You might be able to capture a man for a while, long enough to complicate your life with a baby, and then you'll lose him. Make your own survey of the women around you. See if you can find one who married young and still has her husband. Don't marry until you know he's ready, too.

Men: There is a significant benefit to marrying later in life which I only came to appreciate in retrospect: If you delay marriage long enough to really enjoy the benefits of being a young single man for an extended period, you will be better able to enjoy life as a married man later on. Let me explain why.

As you well know, men in their twenties lead very active lives, and get to enjoy sports and hard work and dating. Once you have a child, however, you will want to give your kid all of your attention and free time, so you can raise a happy child to his/her maximum potential. But, you ask, what about the softball tournament this coming Saturday, and then the back-packing trip next weekend with your buddies? And all the other activities that occupy the time of healthy young bachelors?

Once you are a dad, you will have to give most of these up. You'll have to exchange these for the activities that involve your kid.

The benefit to being an older father when you have your first child is that you no longer care as much about these activities, and you can willingly give them up without any serious feelings of sacrifice. You can devote plenty of time to your new kid, who needs and deserves your attention, without feeling deprived of what used to be the fun things in your life. You don't feel angry at the kid for taking so much of your time, which is what you may have felt if you had become a father too early in your life. You're now ready for full time fatherhood, and you are mature enough to enjoy it completely.

If you recall from the earlier discussion about the cost of marriage, "opportunity cost" is one part of the price you pay for marriage. By getting all of these bachelor-type behaviors out of your system before you settle down to raising kids, you greatly reduce the opportunity cost of marriage.

One hears about middle aged men who leave their wives, dye their hair, get a sports car, and start dating younger women. The ones that I've known who did this were the men who got married too young, and, having never had a young man's bachelorhood, are trying to make up for it later in life. Don't do that. Enjoy your bachelorhood for a long enough time that you won't miss it when it's gone.

14

LIVING TOGETHER

Living together is clearly one of the alternatives to marriage, and it is getting to be prevalent enough to deserve a separate discussion. It is easy to think of circumstances where people might choose not to marry and just want to live together. For instance, younger couples may want to gain the experience of living together even though they are not ready to commit to marriage.

Older couples might decide to just live together in those cases where there is no desire to have children and where marriage might have undesirable legal or financial consequences. And for everybody in between, it may be tempting to take the easy way out to just live together and avoid the finality of marriage.

In this day and age, when state-supported colleges provide co-ed housing, there can't be too much social stigma attached to couples living together. I don't think that this is the issue for most of us. Once you are over twenty one and earning a living, this is not such an unusual experience any more. The important question is whether this is a wise thing to do or not. After giving this a great deal of thought, I have decided that this should be viewed from the sales perspective just like many of the other analogies I have presented in this book. It depends on whether you want to rent, lease or buy.

There are some positive aspects to just living together. Reason One: You still have all your options open, giving you a tremendous feeling of freedom in avoiding all the obligations of marriage. Reason Two: You will both be on your best behavior because you know that either of you can leave at any time. Life should be enjoyable if you can live in an extended courting relationship and you don't argue a lot. Reason Three: Since there won't be any children (hopefully) in this arrangement, you will more likely continue to be interested in sex. Men, in particular, may prefer this arrangement if they think their sex life would suffer if they marry and have kids.

However, for a woman who wants to get married and is trying to evaluate a potential husband, my advice is to not live together until you have a commitment to marriage. My opinion is the result of my experience as a salesman, so let me share this with you.

Most manufacturers build equipment that they hope to sell at a profit and they are not in the business of loaning their equipment. Their customers, if they want this equipment, buy it. Sometimes, however, before making a large investment, a customer will agree to purchase the equipment if they can make the purchase subject to their approval after they have been able to try it out for a while. This is accomplished with what is called an evaluation purchase order. Generally the terms of the evaluation purchase order state that if the product works as advertised, the purchase order stands. That is, in order for the buyer to get out of the deal, he has to show that it didn't work like it was supposed to. He is not allowed to just change his mind and say that he just doesn't want it any more. In these situations, the evaluation period is always short, and clearly specified.

You want the equivalent of the evaluation purchase order, because in most cases the deal will go through. That is, once you have already agreed to marry and have set a date, it might be okay to live together before the wedding if there is some compelling reason to do so. Living together would then simply be an interim condition that leads up to wedding itself. Marriage means making the full investment and buying, whereas living together is analogous to leasing, which doesn't require any serious obligation. Living together allows you to gloss over some of the more difficult issues that face married people, and it doesn't really test you for the compatibility required in a marriage.

For the woman who absolutely wants marriage, the major problem with the live-together situation is that, unless it is the result of a conscious decision process, it has no well defined end to it. It will most likely end when the woman finally decides that the guy is never going to marry her. The price she pays is that during her live-together period she has lost out on opportunities to meet the right man who will marry her. If the objective is to have children, this time lost is more important to the woman than to the man, so it is the woman who has to control her own destiny here.

15

OTHER ALTERNATIVES

I predict that in the future we will see some new kinds of relationships between men and women which will replace our conventional marriage relationships. I base this on my observation of other organizations and how much they have had to change during the last 20 years in order to cope with the realities of our current society. Because people now live so long, it is possible to imagine all kinds of complex emotional and legal relationships that could develop in one's lifetime. When you think about it, you will be an adult for fifty years or so, and it's possible that you will spend long periods in an unmarried status before, after, or between marriages. You would do well to look ahead, with an informed perspective, at your alternatives.

What is marriage anyway? Marriage is a relationship that provides its members with sex, companionship, and a partnership for survival. Marriage entitles you to freedom from intervention in some of your personal affairs, but at the same time obligates you with the responsibility for your mate and the rearing of your children. The reason we all have so much trouble finding an acceptable mate is that it is difficult to find that one very special person who can satisfy all of these needs.

There are lots of people who are lucky enough to find that special person, and they live a long and happy life together. Too many of us, though, either can't find the right mate or too easily discard the one we have.

We were brought up to visualize the typical family as being the "nuclear family", derived from the word nucleus, meaning the center, not the nuclear as in bomb. In this nuclear family, mom and dad and the kids live as a group, insulated from everyone else in the privacy of their own home. Although this has been the model of the family that we all grew up with, it has always been less true that we imagined. Only in the last century, and basically only in the U. S., has a society been wealthy enough to live in this manner. And with divorced and single parents in such high numbers as we have now, even in our current society the nuclear family is more of an ideal than a reality.

Going into the 21st century, the nuclear family was even less prevalent than it was historically. It's likely the family will be further divided by divorce, expanded by remarriage, or even redefined by law. Current divorce rates have been in the fifty percent range for years, which means that many a family that starts out as a nuclear family doesn't stay that way. The extended family of the future may be even more complex than today's, and could include step-relatives, former in-laws, ex-stepparents, etc., in addition to all the more common relatives. Given the many ways modern science now assists in the creation of a child, even the definition of parenthood is changing.

Keep in mind that marriage itself shouldn't be the goal. The goal should be a happy and productive life, and if done right, marriage could be a factor in achieving that goal. It may mean, however that marriage will have to be designed differently. The following ideas may seem crazy now, but as society evolves they may begin to make more sense.

Serial Marriage

Serial marriage seems to be the most common way to solve the problems of modern marriage. If the first marriage doesn't work out, you terminate it after some period of unhappiness and start looking for another mate. A better suited one, you hope, the second time.

The late Margaret Mead, a world renowned anthropologist, liked to say that she married three times, all successfully. Her first husband she referred to as a student-husband. As her career in anthropology progressed, she took another husband who was a traveling partner and interested in her field work. Her third husband was a romantic and intellectual soul mate.

Although this trend has already started, I don't think many will be as lucky as Margaret Mead was. The side effects that result from multiple marriages could be tremendous. Think about the conflicts over household matters, property, inheritance, obligations for care taking, and rivalries for affection. If there are children in both first and second families, problems related to child support payments will make you wish you had done things differently. While there may benefits to serial marriage, it has the potential for making your life very complicated, and expensive.

For some people, there may be a significant change in the way you perceive yourself and what you want out of life as you grow older. In your twenties you may want your mate to be a party animal, whereas a few years later you may want a less volatile relationship and a little more stability. One stewardess told me that after a "roller coaster" first marriage, she had been single for nine years before she found the man that she really wanted. She explained that she didn't really grow up until she was about twenty eight, and in spite of having received some money in her divorce settlement, wishes she had just skipped that first marriage and waited for the second.

Term Marriage

Maybe it would make sense to have marriage last for only five years and then terminate unless it is renewed. Since this is what happens in many marriages anyway, why not be honest about it. Along with the term marriage license, the woman gets a Norplant patch which is an effective five year birth control device. By preventing children in marriages that can't even survive past five years, this alternative would greatly improve the chances of having children who grow up in a two parent family.

Extended Family

It is entirely possible that the laws could change and redefine the family in such a way that a large extended family could incorporate, like a business. This might allow the wealthier family members to transfer funds to other family members without having to pay gift or inheritance taxes, or maybe get tax benefits for helping each other pursue new business ventures. In a large impersonal world where having a network is a big asset, this would improve the success of young adults who have to figure out how to go out and a make a living. Another major benefit is that this larger entity would be in a better position to take care of its members without the need for help from the society at large.

Group Marriage

Another possibility might be a communal living arrangement of some sort or other. Communes have occurred throughout history, some more successful than others, but there are always people trying to come up with a design that works. For the right person under the right circumstances, this might be the most satisfying way to live.

One of these alternative marriage groups that exists in the present was on the Donahue Show to explain what their group was like and how it worked. This group had started with a married couple who invited another couple to join them, and eventually the group grew to include a third couple and several single women. They all lived in a big New England farmhouse with a bunch of kids, some from previous marriages and some from this group. Everybody appeared intelligent, attractive, and well adjusted, including the younger kids who were well behaved during the filming for the show.

Jealousy is apparently not an issue for these people, because they had entered into this relationship voluntarily and could presumably leave at any time. Ownership, personal rights and obligations are totally under their control, so obviously they have worked out an acceptable set of rules and guidelines. Pooling and sharing of resources can be anything they choose it to be, so clearly they have worked that out too.

Before you cross this off as a really screwy marriage, and totally out of the question, consider it from an "organization" point of view. This group has a very well defined procedure for accepting any new member into the group, and the rights and obligations of every member are clearly spelled out. Everybody has to contribute to the group welfare.

Apparently sexual freedom is allowed but never imposed on anyone.

Everyone in the group was allowed to speak out during the show, including some of the older kids, and everyone said the arrangement worked exceedingly well to the satisfaction of everyone in the group. What was interesting was the reaction of Donahue's audience. Without exception, everyone who spoke out or asked a question expressed a negative view of the whole concept. Maybe that was normal, and maybe all of us react negatively to a radical new idea that is thrust upon us with no warning. But we're in no hurry here, so let's think this thing through. Shouldn't we be impressed by an organization that gets the unanimous approval of all its members?

The only big question is what to think about the kids. But first, let's think about the way other kids actually live in our society. In spite of the propaganda about family values and how children ought to be brought up in a stable, loving nuclear family, the fact is that many children aren't that lucky. The papers are full of stories about kids who live in single parent homes, or foster homes, or live in poverty, or suffer from child abuse. Many more are going to face some very uncertain futures because their parents will suffer the loss of employment, or already have. Can anyone really argue that these are better ways to raise children than in a loving, caring household that happens to have multiple care-givers?

Think of the positive environment for the kids. There could always be adults around as baby sitters, trainers, teachers, counselors, and some simply as adult friends and family. This is much like the extended family used to be before our society started separating individual families into single family dwellings. With this many adults helping them learn how to read, monitoring their homework, and helping to keep them out of trouble, wouldn't they have a better start in life than the latch key kids we hear so much about these days who are home alone because the parent(s) work?

From the adults' point of view, this "organization" offers lots of benefits. It is well known that people need close intimate relationships to have a feeling of security and well being, and this format offers multiple close relationships. They employed a very long and careful screening process so that a high level of compatibility and friendship is assured among the members. But this arrangement does not require that any one individual be a perfect match for any other individual, so maintaining this relationship may be easier in some respects than a conventional marriage.

Second, the group could be formed with whatever gender ratio provides the proper balance to satisfy the sexual needs of all the members.

Third, the combined incomes from all of the members, which can be shared in any way they agree upon, can provide a very important safety net for each member. A temporary loss of income by any one member, or an exceptional expense, could be covered with the help of the group. For that matter, it could be agreed that some of the members don't contribute in a monetary fashion at all, and make their contribution some other way.

Clearly this kind of an arrangement is not for everybody, but neither is a conventional marriage, as we are finding out more and more.

Rodger L. Winn

The Winn Quad

Being single is clearly one of the alternatives to marriage, and whether you marry or not, it is highly probable that you will be living single during at least part of your adult life. Unfortunately, although an important part of living is your place of residence, I think that the market has not yet recognized the need for specialized housing for singles. I am convinced that we would greatly improve the quality of life for people who are living single if we were to design a housing environment which I will call a quad.

Throughout history the basic living group for humans has been the family, so it's only natural that housing would be designed to accommodate families. In the U.S., whether the housing is constructed as a house or as an apartment, the floor plans are very similar. Most of the rooms are designed for use by everybody in the family, what we might call common rooms. Only the bedrooms would be considered as private areas, where other people would generally stay out unless they were invited in.

Families are supposed to spend time together, so having a lot of common space which everybody shares makes good sense. Singles, however, don't necessarily want that same kind of constant sharing of space with someone who is only a roommate. Being single doesn't necessarily mean wanting to be alone, however. What you most likely want by being single is a feeling of independence, but not the feeling of loneliness. And of course you want your housing to be affordable. If you analyze our current housing types, you will see that they are not designed to satisfy this set of requirements.

There are housing types that are designed for one person, which include studio apartments, bachelor apartments, and

140

efficiencies. These are lower cost than apartments, but they sacrifice a lot of features in the trade-off. They do satisfy the need for privacy, but they are so separate that they tend to cause the occupant to feel isolated and lonely. Other types of singles housing provide an environment which includes other people, but they sacrifice the privacy that people want and need. This group of housing choices includes dormitories, rooming houses, and rooms rented in someone else's home.

None of these is totally satisfactory in today's environment. If I were single, I'll tell you what kind of a housing choice I would want. I would design a unit with the common area in the center, four bedrooms at the corners, and I would call it a quad. The common area would be shared by the occupants in any way they chose, and this area could be large or small depending on who is designing the quad. Each bedroom would be a larger than normal and would be big enough to allow you to isolate yourself if you felt you needed to be alone. The main difference would be that each bedroom would have its own external entrance for added privacy.

I would envision that a quad could be either stand-alone as a house, or in multiples like an apartment building, and could come in three flavors. The type A quad would have four full bathrooms, one in each unit. Type B would have two bathrooms, each shared by two of the bedrooms. Type C would be the low cost version, and would have a single bathroom shared by all the residents.

A well designed quad would have lots of storage space in the bedrooms and in the common areas, and would have specially designed garages. The other particular features of the quad would depend on the imagination the architect and the level of sophistication and luxury desired by the builder.

Who would want to live in one of these quads? Here are some "roommate" situations that could benefit from this housing arrangement:

1) Four singles. Each could spend as much or as little time with the other members of the quad as he/she desired. Guests could be entertained at the dinner table, in the family room, or in one's private quarters. The benefit is lower rent, some social activity, but plenty of privacy if desired. With four people to share the cost, maybe the quad could even afford maid service now and then.

2) Three singles and one maid. If the income levels of three members were high enough, maybe the three would want to provide the fourth bedroom to someone who would act as maid/cook/housemother. I'm sure there are plenty of older women (or men) who would be delighted to exchange their housekeeping skills for the benefit of a nice housing arrangement like this.

3) One college kid and three senior citizens. In exchange for a reduction in his/her rent, the college kid could do all the running around that is not so easy for the older folks.

4) One health care worker and three invalids. Sharing the cost of a health care provider would certainly make the insurance companies happy.

5) Four single moms with one child each. Child care is one of the most difficult problems faced by single parents these days, and having four women who could share the babysitting task would make life much better for all involved. Schedules could be adjusted so one adult was always home, teaching and playing with the kids. The others could go to work, or school.

A conventional apartment unit in today's environment is not very cost effective, and is usually a big headache for the owner as well as for the tenants. Anyone who is planning to build one might consider building a quad instead. If this arrangement were as popular as I would predict, it might make sense to offer an open ended lease so that anyone could move in or out on short notice. It also might make sense to let the group govern itself and select its own replacements. To assure compatibility and encourage civilized behavior, the lease could include some language which allows the owner to throw out a tenant for any of the standard reasons, or at the request of the other three tenants.

Think of the benefits that the owner of such a housing unit would derive from this new design in housing. If the owner is a live-in, he/she gets three other people to help pay for the mortgage and the taxes. If the owner is an investor, he/she only loses one fourth of the rent when someone moves out. And for the residents, they get a nice mix of privacy and sociability at an affordable price.

My purpose in presenting the quad is to help emphasize that you need to enjoy life as a single so you don't enter into an unfortunate marriage out of frustration or desperation. Being single is a legitimate alternative to marriage, and having the proper housing environment would help make it more acceptable. If you can enjoy life as a single, then you won't want to switch to being married until you're sure that you've found the right person.

The goal is not to marry, but to marry right.

16

CONCLUSION

The laws and customs of our society do not allow anyone to interfere in your decision about whom to select as a mate, or why, or how, and nobody can force you to know what you are doing. However, if you want your marriage to be successful, it will have to satisfy your needs, your partner's needs, and will have to function successfully as an organization. It will take a lot of work, and I think that everybody would benefit from attending special classes to learn about relationships, the differences between men and women, how to please and support each other, how to raise children, etc. In addition, I suggest that you read as many books as possible about how to select a mate and how to make a marriage work. Of the ones I have read, I recommend the following as being enlightening and extremely useful:

Dr. Judith Sills, *How to Stop Looking For Somebody Perfect and Find Someone to Love*

Margaret Kent, *How To Marry The Man Of Your Choice*

Dr. Deborah Tannen, *You Just Don't Understand: Women and Men in Conversation*

Dr. Joyce Brothers, *What Every Woman Should Know About Love and Marriage*

Sharyn Wolf, *50 Ways To Find A Lover*

Linda Sunshine, *Dating Iron John & Other Pleasures*

John Gray, PhD, *Men Are From Mars, Women Are From Venus*

Cris Evat, *Opposite Sides Of The Bed*

Robert Wright, *The Moral Animal: Evolutionary Psychology and Everyday Life*

For many of us, the search for an ideal mate may be a long and arduous process, and success is not guaranteed. Some of the reasons for marriage have changed, and you need to be sure that marriage is what you really want. The marriage relationship is more complex than it ever has been and it will test your abilities more than you can imagine.

Analyze what your own characteristics and preferences are, and look for that special person who is compatible. To help make your search more productive, I suggest that you view yourself as a very critical buyer who has a really big decision to make, and at the same time view yourself as a salesman who has a very special product to sell.

ABOUT THE AUTHOR

Rodger Winn was a high-tech sales engineer for 25 years who thinks that a sales perspective is useful in trying to find and select the perfect mate. He was a successful bachelor for many years until he finally met and married the girl of his dreams. He has analyzed the process he went through and thinks that others could benefit from the lessons he learned. He has been married for 43 years and has two adult sons who also married late (mid and late 30's) and have wonderful marriages.